Pixels and the Politicians

Examining the Impact of Computer Science on Political Campaigns

Ishwar Singh & Rahul Pawar

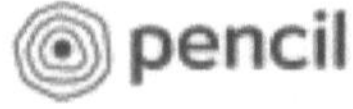

ISBN 978-93-5667-878-1

Published in India 2023 by Pencil

A brand of
One Point Six Technologies Pvt. Ltd.
Unit no. 26, Ground Floor, Building A1,
Wadala Truck Terminal Road,
Near Post Office, Antop Hill, Mumbai - 400037
E connect@thepencilapp.com
W www.thepencilapp.com

Author biography

Ishwar Singh is a distinguished political scientist renowned for his insightful research and significant contributions to the field of political science. Born on February 18, 1992, in a small town in India, Ishwar showed a keen interest in politics and governance from an early age. His fascination with the dynamics of power, decision-making processes, and the impact of politics on society propelled him to pursue a career in political science.

Throughout his career, Ishwar has published numerous influential papers and authored several books on political theory, comparative politics, and public policy. His research has shed light on issues such as democratic governance, political ideologies, social movements, and the impact of globalization on politics. His insightful analysis and ability to connect theoretical frameworks with real-world phenomena have earned him acclaim within the academic community.

Apart from his academic pursuits, Ishwar has also been actively involved in policy advocacy and consulting. His expertise and insights have been sought after by government agencies, international organizations, and non-profit organizations alike. He has served as a consultant on various projects, providing strategic guidance on policy formulation and implementation.

Ishwar Singh's contributions to the field of political science have been widely recognized. He has received numerous accolades and awards for his outstanding research and teaching. His work has not only advanced the academic understanding of political science but has also influenced policymakers and practitioners in their decision-making processes.

Rahul Pawar is a distinguished computer scientist who has made significant contributions to the field of computer science and technology. Born on July 15, 1986, Rahul displayed a passion for computers and technology from an early age. His curiosity and enthusiasm for understanding how things work and solving complex problems led him to pursue a career in computer science.

After completing his formal education, Rahul embarked on a career as a computer scientist, dedicating himself to research and development. He joined a prominent technology company, where he worked on cutting-edge projects that pushed the boundaries of innovation. Rahul's expertise in machine learning and artificial intelligence allowed him to make significant breakthroughs in the development of intelligent systems and algorithms.

Rahul's research and inventions have had a profound impact on various domains, including healthcare, finance, and robotics. He has published numerous research papers in esteemed journals, sharing his findings and advancements with the scientific community. His work has focused on leveraging machine learning techniques to solve complex problems, improve decision-making processes, and enhance the efficiency of systems.

CONTENTS

Epigraph

"Technology has evolved into the most potent political force of our time, permanently altering the political landscape. The fascinating investigation of the complex connection between computer science and democracy provided by Pixels and Politicians reveals the incredible influence of technology on our political institutions. Understanding the relationship between politicians and pixels in this digital era is crucial for ensuring the democracy's future."

Foreword

The convergence of computer science and politics has grown in significance in the era of fast technological development. The manner in which political campaigns are run have undergone a fundamental transition as our society gets more and more digital. Computer science has become a significant player in influencing how politics is shaped, from voter engagement tactics to the gathering and analysis of enormous quantities of data.

In "Pixels and Politicians: Examining the Impact of Computer Science on Political Campaigns," we set out on an exciting quest to discover this dynamic connection. We explore the many ways that computer science has transformed politics, altering campaign tactics, voter outreach, and even the fundamental essence of democracy itself, via the pages of this stimulating book.

Since their origin, political campaigns have seen substantial change. A digital revolution has replaced the days of only depending on conventional grassroots organization, door-to-door canvassing, and town hall meetings. Modern political campaigns make use of cutting-edge tools and creative strategies to reach a larger audience, create impactful messages, and enlist supporters. Computer technology has set the ground for transformational changes in the way politicians and their teams approach their campaigns, from social media platforms to big data analytics.

It is impossible to understate the influence of social media on contemporary politics. The dynamics of political communication have been significantly changed by the emergence of websites like Facebook, Twitter, and Instagram. Politicians have never previously had such direct access to the public, allowing them to communicate with voters immediately and on a personal basis. Political campaigns now have to contend with both possibilities and obstacles as a result of the influence of viral campaigns, internet financing, and targeted advertising.

Furthermore, the age of data-driven politics was ushered in by computer science. In order to assess voter behavior, pinpoint the most important concerns, and target their message to certain groups, campaigns now primarily depend on advanced data analytics. Campaigns may develop highly individualized and targeted voter engagement tactics by evaluating large amounts of data gathered from multiple sources. Success of a campaign now heavily depends on how well this data is used, which has led to worries about privacy, ethics, and the possibility of manipulation.

This book's pages are filled with fascinating case examples that show how computer technology may significantly alter political campaigns. We will see how cutting-edge data analytics influenced election results, how political debate has migrated to social media, and how emerging technologies like artificial intelligence and machine learning are being used to forecast voter behavior and improve campaign tactics. We learn more about the potential and difficulties that exist at the nexus of computer science and politics thanks to these gripping accounts.

In addition to shedding insight on the revolutionary impact of computer science on political campaigns, "Pixels and Politicians" also raises significant concerns on the moral implications of these developments. We need to address concerns about data use that is ethical, transparent, and respects privacy. It is crucial that we critically assess how new technologies affect democratic processes to make sure that they do not jeopardize the very foundational values of our political institutions.

Readers who embark on this intellectual journey will be well-equipped to negotiate the challenging terrain of computer science in political campaigns. They will learn about the tactics used by campaigns, the digital world's shaping algorithms, and the effects these innovations have on society as a whole. As a compass, "Pixels and Politicians" leads us through the complexities of this changing environment and encourages us to think about the ramifications for our democracy.

I'd like to conclude by extending an invitation to you to take this illuminating trip through the pages of "Pixels and Politicians: Examining the Impact of Computer Science on Political Campaigns." You will come to really appreciate the transformational potential of computer science in the field of politics as you go through the next chapters. This book serves as a reminder that, just as technology is always changing, so too must our comprehension of how it affects our democratic procedures. We can only make sure that the impact of computer science on political campaigns continues to be a force for good change by having educated conversations and encouraging ethical behavior.

Birinder Pal Kaur

Preface

A thorough investigation of the changing link between technology, especially computer science, and politics is provided in Pixels and Politicians: Examining the Impact of Computer Science on Political Campaigns. This book aims to decipher the complex web that links technology, politics, and society in an age dominated by digital breakthroughs and the growing impact of social media.

Politicians now communicate with voters, design messages, and win elections in whole new ways as a result of the fusion of computer science and politics. Campaign tactics, fundraising methods, voter targeting, and even policy drafting have all undergone revolutionary changes as a result of the unparalleled availability to data and the development of powerful algorithms. Computer technology has an indisputable impact on politics and has drastically changed the political environment.

In-depth exploration of the many facets of this transformational interaction is the goal of this book. It aims to provide a thorough overview of how computer technology has influenced political campaigns, from the macro-level of electoral systems to the micro-level of individual voter interactions. To provide readers a more in-depth knowledge of the complex processes at work, we explore case studies, empirical research, and theoretical frameworks.

This book's chapters are arranged topically to address the many facets of computer science's influence on political campaigns. We start by looking at the development of digital campaigning and how conventional campaign techniques have changed. We look at how candidates use social media, data analytics, and machine learning algorithms to organize support, target voters, and alter public opinion.

We explore the role of computer technology in promoting citizen involvement and participation outside of the political arena. We examine the growth of online discussion tools, crowdsourcing efforts, and e-democracy platforms that let individuals actively participate in politics. We also look at the potential and problems that new technologies like blockchain, AI, and VR provide for promoting open decision-making and transparent government.

The ethical ramifications of the increasing use of computer technology in political campaigns are being severely examined. We look at topics like algorithmic bias, data protection, privacy, and the weaponization of information. The book explores the moral conundrums that politicians, campaign strategists, and technologists have while managing the intricate interface between politics and technology.

We examine how computer science has impacted election processes, voting patterns, and democratic institutions as a whole, in addition to the effect on political campaigns themselves. We look at how technology may be used to improve accessibility, accuracy, and election management. Additionally, we look at the difficulties of safeguarding elections in the digital world and reducing the dangers of cyberattacks and misinformation campaigns.

Finally, the goal of this book is to start a discussion on the direction that computer science will take in politics in the future. We look at new patterns and make predictions about the possible effects of upcoming technological developments like quantum computing, augmented reality, and the internet of things. We want to motivate politicians, technologists, and people to actively influence the future of technology in the political domain by reflecting on the opportunities and dangers that lie ahead.

A broad spectrum of readers, including academics, researchers, practitioners, policymakers, and anyone interested in the nexus between technology and politics, are intended for Pixels and Politicians: Examining the Impact of Computer Science on Political Campaigns. By exploring the intricacies, potential, and difficulties of this quickly developing topic, we want to add to the continuing discussion about how computer science influences our political results and democratic processes.

As we begin our investigation, we cordially welcome readers to accompany us on an exciting tour of the contemporary political digital world. The pages that follow provide a complex tapestry of observations, analyses, and thoughts with the goal of illuminating the significant changes occurring where politicians and pixels converge.

Ishwar Singh

Rahul Pawar

Acknowledgements

We would like to express our sincere gratitude and appreciation to our beloved parents, Smt. Amarjit Kaur, Shri Pal Singh, Smt. Saroj Pawar, and Shri Tilak Pawar, for their unfailing support, love, and encouragement during our journey to research and write this thesis on "Pixels and Politicians: Examining the Impact of Computer Science on Political Campaigns." Our success has been greatly aided by their advice and support, and we will always be grateful to them for their tremendous efforts.

First and foremost, we want to express our gratitude to Smt. Amarjit Kaur and Smt. Saroj Pawar, our moms. Our lives have been supported by their love and sacrifice. They have consistently served as our pillars of support, inspiration, and comprehension. Our ability to overcome obstacles and achieve our academic goals has been fueled by their unwavering support and faith in our skills.

We owe a debt of appreciation to our dads, Shri Pal Singh and Shri Tilak Pawar, for their priceless advice and knowledge. They have continuously served as an inspiration to us, showing us the value of tenacity, diligence, and commitment. Our paths and aspirations have been significantly shaped and nurtured by their constant support and faith in our goals.

We also want to express our gratitude to our parents for giving up things in order to provide us the greatest educational opportunity. To make sure we had access to high-quality education and resources, they worked diligently and even made personal sacrifices. Our strong feeling of appreciation and desire to live up to their standards have been inspired by their selflessness and devotion.

We are appreciative of our parents for creating a culture that values education and curiosity. They fostered our intellectual development from an early age, motivating us to look into new concepts, challenge the existing quo, and become passionate about learning. Their unshakable faith in the value of education has helped to mold us into critical thinkers and lifelong learners.

Additionally, we would want to express our sincere gratitude for the many sacrifices our parents have made in order to provide for us materially, morally, and emotionally. They have always been our pillars of support, providing direction in trying times and exulting in our victories as no one else can. Their unshakable faith in our competence has given us the courage to follow our aspirations bravely.

We also want to thank our parents for their incredible tolerance and understanding during this process. They have given advice, been a listening ear, and given the emotional support required to go through the highs and lows of academic research. Even in our self-doubt, their confidence in us has been a tremendous source of support.

We also like to thank our parents for their support and interest in our academic endeavors. Our research interests have been significantly shaped by their constant encouragement to investigate new areas, participate in thought-provoking debates, and pursue greatness. Our enthusiasm for examining how computer science affects political campaigns has been stoked by their faith in the ability of education to bring about good change.

For their incalculable contributions to our life and this thesis, our parents, Smt. Amarjit Kaur, Shri Pal Singh, Smt. Saroj Pawar, and Shri Tilak Pawar, deserve the deepest gratitude. This scientific project would not have been feasible without their unfailing support, love, and advice. They have been a continual source of inspiration and strength in our lives. We dedicate this thesis to our parents in appreciation of the tireless work they did to mold us into the people we are today. May we always strive to honor them in whatever we do.

Pixels and the Politicians

Chapter 1

Introduction

1. Introduction

Technology has become a potent force in the quickly changing world of contemporary politics, influencing how political campaigns are conducted and elections are decided. Computer science, a discipline that has changed businesses and political campaigns alike, is at the vanguard of this technological transformation. "Pixels and Politicians" dives into this interesting nexus, examining how computer technology has altered how politicians interact with their voters and changed the dynamics of political campaigns.

The widespread use of the internet and the expansion of social media have profoundly changed how political ideas are communicated, understood, and acted upon in the digital age. Politicians may now successfully target certain populations and grasp voter preferences because to the strong tools and methods developed by computer science to tame the massive volumes of data produced online.

Data analytics and predictive modeling have become more popular, which is one of computer science's most noteworthy effects on political campaigns. Campaign strategists can examine massive datasets, find hidden trends, and make data-driven choices thanks to cutting-edge algorithms and machine learning approaches. As a consequence, campaigns may better tailor their message, fundraising efforts, and voter outreach, making them more effective.

Furthermore, communication and mobilization tactics have been transformed by computer science. Politicians now engage in virtual combat on social media platforms to get attention, influence public opinion, and build support. Computer technology has given politicians access to previously unheard-of channels for connecting with people and fostering grassroots movements, from viral films and convincing advertising campaigns to real-time constituent contact.

However, there are difficulties and ethical issues with the influence of computer science on political campaigns. Intense discussions regarding the responsible and ethical use of technology in politics have been triggered by concerns about data privacy, misinformation, and the possibility of algorithmic bias. Examining the possible effects and protections is essential to ensuring fair and transparent election processes as campaigns grow more dependent on algorithms and automated decision-making systems.

In "Pixels and Politicians" we will explore the many facets of this quickly developing area. We will investigate case studies, look at technical developments, and critically evaluate the social effects of computer science on political campaigns via an interdisciplinary perspective. By doing this, we want to shed light on the intricate relationship between politicians and pixels, providing knowledge about political campaigns' present and future in a society that is becoming more and more computerized.

The book "Pixels and Politicians" also aims to discuss the wider ramifications and effects of this technological revolution. As computer science develops at an unparalleled rate, it has a greater impact on political campaigns than just tactics and strategy. The nature of democracy, the influence of technology on public opinion, and the possibility for digital manipulation are all addressed in great detail.

The practice of microtargeting is one of the major topics covered in this book. Political campaigns may now target certain people or groups with messages based on their online activity, tastes, and demographics thanks to the development of sophisticated data analytics. The political process is significantly impacted by this degree of accuracy because it enables politicians to engage with people in echo chambers and to reinforce preexisting prejudices.

Furthermore, cybersecurity is impacted by computer science in terms of political campaigns. Campaigns are more open to online threats and hacking attempts due to their digitalization and dependence on technology for data storage and communication. In a time of rising cybersecurity dangers, the book explores the difficulties of securing election systems, preserving private information, and maintaining the integrity of the democratic process.

Additionally, "Pixels and Politicians" investigates the moral issues related to the use of artificial intelligence (AI) in political campaigns. Virtual assistants and chatbots powered by AI have proliferated as popular methods for interacting with voters, but they also raise concerns about accountability and transparency. The book offers suggestions for mitigating possible biases and prejudice as well as a critical analysis of the ethical frameworks that should govern the use of AI in political situations.

Last but not least, "Pixels and Politicians" explores the international aspect of computer science in political campaigns. It explores the disparities in techniques, rules, and cultural ramifications as other nations and political systems accept and adapt technology innovations. The book provides a comprehensive knowledge of the complicated interaction between computer science and politics in diverse socio-political circumstances by exploring case studies from various countries.

In conclusion, the study "Pixels and Politicians: Examining the Impact of Computer Science on Political Campaigns" goes beyond a cursory examination of digital campaign strategies. It explores how computer technology has profoundly changed political campaigns, creating both possibilities and difficulties. The book aims to give readers a thorough understanding of the impact of computer science on the political landscape, encouraging critical discussions and well-informed decision-making in this increasingly digital era. This is done by looking at the ethical, societal, and global dimensions of this intersection.

1.1 Introducing the convergence of computer science and politics

Politics and computer science coming together is a major development in the contemporary age. Computer science has a presence in politics due to the quick development of technology and the growing influence of data on our communities. This convergence has changed the way we think about political processes by creating new opportunities for analysis, decision-making, and governance.

In data analytics and predictive modeling, computer science has had a significant influence on politics. It is now possible to use the enormous quantity of data produced by numerous sources, including social media, internet platforms, and government databases, to gather insightful knowledge about voter behavior, public mood, and political trends. Political actors may modify their methods to enhance their chances of success by using advanced algorithms and machine learning approaches.

Additionally, computer technology has aided in the creation of online tools and platforms that improve political involvement and participation. Citizens now have better access to political information thanks to the usage of social media, online forums, and mobile apps, allowing them to express their ideas, organize grassroots movements, and hold elected officials responsible. By bridging the gap between the public and political institutions, these technological developments have promoted a more inclusive and participatory democracy.

Political and computer science convergence has also sparked significant ethical and legal concerns. Concerns regarding privacy, data security, and public opinion manipulation have risen as data becomes a more lucrative resource in political campaigns. A critical concern for both politicians and technologists is safeguarding the integrity of democratic processes and the appropriate use of data. Utilizing the advantages of computer technology while reducing possible hazards requires striking the ideal balance between innovation and regulation.

In addition, the fusion of computer technology and politics has spawned new academic specialties. For instance, computational social science analyzes large-scale social events and political processes by fusing computing approaches with social science theory. This multidisciplinary approach has produced insightful information on issues including political networks, polarization, and the dissemination of false information. We can better comprehend the intricate interaction between politics and technology by bringing together specialists from a variety of sectors, and we can create effective methods for solving social concerns.

A new era of political participation and decision-making has begun as a result of the intersection of computer science and politics. Computer science has significantly impacted politics via multidisciplinary research, internet platforms, and data analytics. This confluence has enormous benefits, but it also has significant cultural, legal, and ethical ramifications that must be carefully considered. We can develop a more informed, participatory, and inclusive political system by embracing this confluence and wisely using technology.

1.2 The increasing role of technology in political campaigns

The way political parties and politicians interact with people, acquire information, and organize support has changed as a result of the growing use of technology in political campaigns. Technology improvements in recent years have made it possible for campaigns to use a variety of tools and platforms to reach a larger audience, customize their message, and improve their campaign techniques. The use of social media, big data analytics, targeted advertising, and grassroots organizing are just a few of the many ways that technology has impacted political campaigns.

The development of social media as a potent campaign weapon is one of the biggest transformations brought about by technology. Social media sites like Facebook, Twitter, and Instagram have completely changed how politicians interact with the general population. Candidates can promote their thoughts, gather supporters, and respond to controversies immediately thanks to the direct lines of contact they provide. Additionally, social media platforms have democratized political discourse by enabling people to participate in political debates, express their viewpoints, and launch grassroots initiatives. Due to this accessibility, candidates have been able to establish and organize sizable online communities, fostering a feeling of connection and participation that was not feasible via conventional campaigning techniques.

The use of big data analytics is a crucial component of technology in political campaigns. Campaigns may examine voter behavior, preferences, and demographics using the massive quantities of data accessible today in order to customize their messaging and tactics. Campaigns may use data analytics to locate swing votes, target certain demographics, and distribute tailored information. This data-driven strategy improves campaigns' efficiency and efficacy while also enabling more precise messaging. Campaigns may create messages that resonate and increase participation by studying the issues and preferences of various voter groups.

Modern political campaigns now include targeted advertising as a crucial component. Online platforms have very complex advertising capabilities, enabling campaigns to precisely target certain demographics. Campaigns may provide customized adverts to prospective voters based on their interests, geography, and online activity by using user data and sophisticated targeting algorithms. With a tailored strategy, communications are delivered to the desired audience, maximizing the effect of campaign investment. Digital advertising also has the benefit of real-time monitoring and performance evaluation, which enables campaigns to optimize their expenditure and change their strategy in response to data insights.

Additionally, technology has transformed volunteerism and community organization. Now, campaigns may more effectively recruit, prepare, and organize volunteers by using digital tools and platforms. Volunteers may easily sign up, access information, and contact with campaign officials thanks to mobile apps and web platforms. Technology also enables the gamification of volunteerism, which encourages participation and fosters a feeling of community. These technologies have increased the effect and reach of grassroots initiatives by allowing campaigns to efficiently organize a huge number of volunteers and supporters.

Technology has numerous advantages for political campaigns, but it also has drawbacks and causes for worry. The possibility for inaccurate information and the propagation of false news are two important causes for worry. False or incorrect information may more easily spread quickly via social media platforms, gaining popularity and swaying public opinion. To address this problem and maintain the legitimacy of the political process, a mix of technology solutions, media literacy initiatives, and responsible platform regulations are needed.

Furthermore, concerns regarding privacy and data protection are raised by the use of technology in political campaigns. Discussions concerning ethical standards and the possibility of misuse have been triggered by the acquisition and use of personal data for political reasons. Maintaining a balance between using data for successful campaigning and upholding people's right to privacy is a constant struggle that requires strong legislation and transparency measures.

As a result of technology playing a larger part in political campaigns, there has been a significant change in how politicians interact with people, collect information, and organize support. Social media platforms have transformed communication, enabling candidates to engage voters and reach a broader audience. Campaigns may adjust their plans and messaging to target voter groups using big data analytics, and focused advertising increases the effectiveness of campaign investment. Technology helps campaigns organize supporters more successfully by facilitating volunteerism and grassroots organization. However, to guarantee the integrity of the democratic process in the digital era, issues like the dissemination of false information and worries about privacy and data protection must be addressed.

Chapter 2

Evolution of Political Campaigns

2. Introduction

Political campaigns have undergone a remarkable transformation that has been reflected in the shifting dynamics of society, technology, and communication. Political campaigns have evolved throughout history from simple attempts at persuasion to intricate and highly sophisticated operations. The important advancements and their effects on the election process will be highlighted as this article examines the significant turning points in the history of political campaigns.

Political campaigns in the past were mostly based on interpersonal connections and public speaking. Leading figures would visit various areas, speaking to audiences and outlining their ideal system of government. Due to their reliance on in-person interaction and word of mouth, these campaigns had a restricted audience and were ineffective. However, they laid the groundwork for the significance of communication and public perception in political campaigns.

A new age of political campaigning started in the 15th century with the invention of the printing press. Political candidates were able to reach a broader audience by using pamphlets and broadsheets to spread their beliefs. This innovation transformed the reach and effect of political campaigns by enabling politicians to focus their message on certain areas and demographic groups. Political parties were also made possible by the printing press since their ideology could be spread via printed materials.

Technology made major strides in the 20th century, which profoundly changed political campaigns. A new age of mass communication began with the invention of radio and television. Millions of people may now hear political candidates' live speeches, interviews, and commercials. While television added charm and visual appeal to the political scene, radio enabled politicians to reach people directly in their homes. Campaign tactics changed as a result, with politicians putting more emphasis on soundbites and image-building.

Political campaigns underwent another change in the late 20th century with the emergence of the internet and digital media. Candidates have a previously unheard-of platform to interact with people, disseminate information, and raise money online. Websites become essential campaign tools by providing a centralized location for supporters to acquire information about candidates, their stance on issues, and ways to donate. The development of email and web advertising as economical communication channels allowed for focused marketing to certain segments.

The 21st century saw the emergence of social media platforms as paradigm shifters. Social media sites such as Facebook, Twitter, and Instagram changed the way political campaigns were run. Through social media networks, candidates may now engage with people directly, provide real-time information, and mobilize support. Social media's ability to become viral allows for the quick dissemination of political ideas, affecting public opinion and igniting grassroots movements. This change also led to the democratization of political campaigns since it allowed even candidates with little financial means to become visible and engage voters.

Political campaigns have faced difficulties as they have evolved. The problem of false information and fake news is one of the key worries in contemporary campaigns. Digital platforms make it simple to share information, which makes it easy for false narratives to spread and sway public opinion. The challenging terrain of fact-checking, media literacy, and stopping the spread of misinformation must now be negotiated by political campaigns.

Additionally, worries regarding privacy and ethical ramifications have been highlighted by the rising dependence on data analytics and targeted advertising. Large volumes of personal data are now available to political campaigns, enabling them to target specific voters with messaging and adverts. This raises concerns about the propriety of exploiting people's data for political purposes and the risk of manipulation.

Future developments in artificial intelligence (AI) and machine learning are expected to influence how political campaigns are run. Massive quantities of data can be analyzed, voter behavior can be predicted, and campaign tactics can be optimized using AI-powered algorithms. Virtual assistants (VAs) and chatbots may become crucial components of political campaigns by offering voters individualized interactions and information. To guarantee openness, accountability, and justice in the use of AI in political campaigns, ethical issues must be taken into account.

Cultural, technical, and communication improvements have spurred the dynamic growth of political campaigns. Political campaigns have evolved to new channels and techniques to reach and engage people from ancient civilizations to the digital era. Emerging technologies will probably continue to influence how political campaigns are run in the future, necessitating careful consideration of their ethical ramifications and the upholding of democratic norms.

2.1 Historical overview of political campaigns

The development of democratic societies and the course of history have both been significantly influenced by political campaigns. Political campaigns have been used as venues for politicians to express their views, interact with voters, and compete for political power from ancient civilizations to contemporary democracies. This historical review tries to examine how political campaigns have evolved through time, emphasizing significant turning points, essential tactics, and the effects they have had on the political environment.

Ancient civilizations like the Greek and Roman Republic city-states and their city-states may be used as a starting point to understand the origins of political campaigning. Political candidates would make speeches at the Agora in Athens, renowned as the cradle of democracy, in an effort to influence voters to cast their ballots in their favor. Early campaigns emphasized oratorical prowess, personal magnetism, and promises of better administration. In the Roman Republic, prospective politicians would canvass and give speeches in front of crowds to win support and win elected offices.

Political campaigning was less prevalent throughout the medieval age, which was defined by feudal systems and kingdoms, as a result of the demise of ancient civilizations. However, political involvement returned throughout the Renaissance era. The invention of the printing press in the 15th century altered the way that knowledge was shared by making political pamphlets and treatises more publicly available. The forerunners of contemporary campaign strategies, like Machiavelli in Italy and Thomas Paine in the American colonies, used these platforms to promote political change.

Political parties grew in popularity and modern democracy was born in the 18th and 19th centuries. Early republican presidential elections in the United States witnessed the rise of grassroots groups, public demonstrations, and the use of media to affect public opinion. Important campaigns, like Andrew Jackson's in 1828, concentrated on enlisting the support of the general public, signaling a departure from the elitist strategy of previous political campaigns. Political slogans and posters also became popular during this time period, using visual interest and clear language to draw in voters.

Mass media made great strides in the 20th century, significantly altering political campaigns. Candidates were more easily able to reach a wider audience once radio and then television were invented. Kennedy's polished demeanor and charm won over viewers in the first televised presidential debate between him and Richard Nixon in 1960, highlighting the effectiveness of television as a weapon for political campaigns. Political image-building and advertising thereafter became crucial elements of campaigns, highlighting the significance of media management and visual communication.

Political campaigns underwent another transformation with the introduction of the internet and other digital technologies in the late 20th century. The emergence of social media sites like Facebook and Twitter made it possible for candidates to communicate with voters directly, disseminate messages, and organize supporters. It is generally recognized that Barack Obama's presidential campaign in 2008 marked a turning point in the use of social media to attract young people and create a grassroots movement. Candidates were able to focus their messaging to certain demographics because to the use of data analytics and targeted web advertising.

Political campaigns have particular difficulties even if they have adapted to the digital era. The spread of false information and "fake news" has eroded public confidence and made the communication environment more challenging. A complex network of social media algorithms, filter bubbles, and echo chambers must now be navigated by campaigns. In addition, the gathering and use of voter data raises issues of privacy and ethics.

Future-looking technology might once again transform political campaigns, including artificial intelligence and virtual reality. Virtual reality might provide immersive experiences for voters to connect with politicians on a deeper level, while AI-driven computers could analyze enormous quantities of data to build highly individualized campaign plans. But it's important to carefully evaluate ethical issues like privacy, transparency, and the impact of technology on democracy.

Political campaigns have changed throughout time in response to social shifts and technical developments. Campaigns have used a variety of tactics to alter public opinion and win political power from the time of ancient Greece to the present, including oratory skills, written media, television, and internet platforms. In order to ensure that political campaigns continue to promote informed participation, inclusiveness, and a lively democratic process, it is crucial to look back at the past while embracing the future.

2.2 Traditional campaign strategies and techniques

Political candidates, organizations, and corporations have long used conventional campaign methods and tactics to spread messages, sway public opinion, and achieve desired results. These tactics include a wide variety of actions, from neighborhood initiatives to public relations campaigns, and they have developed through time to accommodate shifting social dynamics and technological advancements. We shall go into the numerous facets of conventional campaign strategies and tactics in this article, examining their essential elements and their influence on public discourse and decision-making.

The creation of a thorough campaign strategy is one of the core components of conventional campaign tactics. This strategy acts as a road map for the campaign, detailing the objectives, target market, message, methods, and timetable. Finding the main concerns, voting demographics, and possible supporters or clients needs thorough study and analysis. Strategists may craft their ideas and strategies to appeal to their target audience by knowing the environment in which the campaign runs.

Grassroots mobilization is a key tactic in conventional campaign techniques. In order to generate support and a surge of passion, this strategy requires interacting with people locally. Door-to-door canvassing, phone banking, planning neighborhood events, and creating volunteer networks are a few examples of grassroots activities. These initiatives seek to foster a feeling of civic engagement, giving people the tools they need to promote the campaign's message and rally their social networks.

Media relations are another crucial component of conventional campaign strategy. Public opinion is greatly influenced by media coverage, which reaches a large audience. One way to get media attention is through establishing contacts with journalists, writing press releases, and setting up press conferences. There are options to spread campaign themes and address detractors or opponents via conventional media venues including newspapers, television, and radio. Campaigns may control their story and preserve a favorable public image with the aid of adept media management.

Advertising is a potent weapon used in conventional campaigns in addition to media relations. In order to engage the target audience in advertising efforts, captivating visual and audio material is often produced. Traditional campaign advertising often takes the shape of billboards, print and radio ads, television and radio commercials, and direct mail campaigns. In order to convince voters or customers to support the candidate or buy the product, it is important to raise name recognition, emphasize important policy stances or product attributes.

Another crucial element of conventional campaign strategy is public speaking and rallies. At public gatherings and rallies, candidates and campaign spokespeople typically give speeches to connect with supporters, lay out their platform, and energize the base. Candidates may use these occasions to demonstrate their charm, leadership skills, and policy stances. Successful public speaking may motivate and enthuse audience members, igniting excitement and gaining momentum for the movement.

Traditional campaign tactics also often use surrogates or endorsers. Surrogates are those who promote a campaign or a product on a candidate's or an organization's behalf. They could be public officials, well-known people, or authorities in a certain area. Endorsements from well-known, reputable personalities may increase credibility, broaden reach, and influence customers or voters who are still debating a purchase.

Another common method for interacting with voters or customers directly is door-to-door campaigning. Volunteers or paid personnel from the campaign make personal visits to residences or places of business to speak with people, respond to inquiries, and hand out information. By allowing for tailored encounters, this tactic enables campaigns to address particular issues and create bonds with prospective supporters or clients.

Additionally, conventional campaign techniques often entail holding focus groups and surveys to collect information and gauge public reaction. These research techniques provide insightful information on consumer or voter preferences, assisting campaigns in honing their messaging, identifying important concerns, and customizing their plans appropriately. Campaigns may successfully shape their ideas and policies to connect with the public by knowing the issues and priorities of their target audience.

Traditional campaign tactics have a few drawbacks even if they have a long history of success. They may be costly, needing large sums of money to support marketing initiatives, employ personnel, and plan events.

Additionally, conventional approaches often focus on one-way communication, with campaigns conveying information to the public rather than encouraging meaningful interaction or discourse. In an age of social media and digital engagement, when two-way communication and online grassroots mobilization have gained significance, this constraint has grown more and more obvious.

In conclusion, conventional political and commercial campaigns have relied heavily on tried-and-true approaches and strategies for decades. Traditional campaigns include elements like grassroots organizing, media relations, advertising, public speaking, endorsements, door-to-door campaigning, and research techniques. While these tactics have changed throughout time to include new media and technological platforms, they still affect public debate and have a significant impact on decision-making. But at a time of digital revolution and shifting social dynamics, conventional campaign tactics must be supported with cutting-edge techniques that make the most of online interaction and communication.

2.3 The advent of technology in campaigns and its transformative effect

With the introduction of technology, political campaigns have undergone a tremendous metamorphosis. Political campaigns have grabbed the chance to use technology to their advantage as technological developments continue to influence our society. Technology has fundamentally changed the way political campaigns are run, transforming time-honored practices like door-to-door canvassing and print ads into cutting-edge strategies like social media marketing and data analytics. The disruptive impact of technology on political campaigns will be examined in this article, along with its consequences for communication, mobilization, voter involvement, financing, and targeting.

The revolution in communication is one of technology's most profound effects on political campaigns. There are now more ways than ever for political candidates to communicate with people directly because to the growth of the internet, social media platforms, and mobile devices. Politicians now use social media sites like Facebook, Twitter, and Instagram as effective tools to spread their message, interact with followers, and sway public opinion. These platforms allow for direct communication between politicians and voters, dismantling boundaries and encouraging a feeling of community. Technology has also made it possible for campaign staff, volunteers, and voters to communicate quickly and effectively, allowing extensive coordination. Examples of these technologies include email, instant messaging, and video conferencing.

The way campaigns recruit supporters and participate in grassroots activity has also changed as a result of technology. People may now organize themselves, build groups, and plan activities for a common goal thanks to online platforms. These platforms may now be used by campaigns to organize rallies, gather volunteers, and raise awareness of events. Additionally, crowdfunding platforms have transformed fundraising by enabling initiatives to harness the strength of group donations from a significant number of people. This has made campaign fundraising more democratic and less reliant on conventional funding sources.

With the use of new communication channels made possible by technology, campaigns may now target certain populations with messages and tactics that are more relevant to them. Campaigns may pinpoint the important problems that matter to various voter groups using data analytics and voter profile tools, and then create customized communications that speak to those groups. Additionally, interactive websites, mobile apps, and online polls help campaigns obtain voter input, comprehend their preferences, and effectively address their problems. This two-way dialogue between campaigns and voters raises involvement, encourages diversity, and improves voter engagement.

Technology's development has revolutionized political campaign fundraising and donor outreach. Campaigns may now more easily reach a larger audience thanks to online platforms, which enables them to draw tiny contributions from supporters all around the globe. With the use of social media sharing and viral marketing, campaigns may now construct interesting and unique online fundraising campaigns that broaden their audience. Additionally, campaigns may analyze donor behavior, find future donors, and customize fundraising techniques to enhance donor outreach and engagement thanks to donor management systems and analytics tools.

Campaigns may now use data analytics and customized advertising to maximize their outreach efforts thanks to technology. Campaigns are able to learn more about the demographics, voting patterns, and behavior of voters by gathering and analyzing enormous volumes of data. With the use of this data, campaigns may target certain demographic groups with advertising and content that will have the most effect. Additionally, the precise targeting capabilities provided by digital advertising platforms allow campaigns to contact voters based on characteristics like age, geography, hobbies, and political affiliations. The efficacy of political message is improved, and there is a greater chance that voters may change their minds.

While there is no denying that technology has had a transformational impact on campaigns, there are several difficulties and moral issues to be aware of. Careful consideration must be given to problems including data privacy, false information, algorithmic biases, and the digital divide. Maintaining the integrity of the political process and safeguarding democratic norms depend on the ethical and appropriate use of technology in campaigns. To guarantee that everyone has equal access to campaign information and participation, campaigns must be honest about their data collecting and use procedures, take action to stop the spread of false information, and try to close the digital gap.

Technology has profoundly changed how political campaigns communicate, organize, interact with people, generate money, and focus their efforts. This new era of political campaigning is the result. The strength of technology rests in its capacity to facilitate direct communication between politicians and voters, foster grassroots movement, raise voter turnout, change financing, and allow data-driven and focused marketing tactics. But immense power also entails great responsibility. In order to achieve a future where technology is used for the greater benefit of democracy, supporting openness, inclusion, and public involvement, campaigns must manage the ethical issues and hurdles presented by technology.

Chapter 3

The Rise of Computer Science

3. Introduction

Over the last century, computer science has been on an amazing excursion that has profoundly changed the world. Computer science has evolved from a small, specialized field into a hub of knowledge and creativity. The emergence of computer science is examined in this article along with its development, significant discoveries, and social effects. We may acquire a thorough knowledge of how computer science has influenced the current world by looking at significant advancements and notable personalities.

The necessity for automated computations and data processing led to the development of computer science. In the 19th century, pioneers like Charles Babbage and Ada Lovelace lay the groundwork for the creation of computers. However, computer science did not become acknowledged as a separate branch of study until the middle of the 20th century. The groundwork for a transformational journey was laid with the development of the electronic computer and the founding of the first computer science departments.

An important turning point in the development of computer science was the advent of modern computing. In the 1940s, the ENIAC, the first general-purpose electronic computer, was created. The revolutionary transistor was then created in the 1950s. These developments transformed the field of computing, enabling faster, more dependable, and more widely available computers. More individuals were able to access the power of computers thanks to the introduction of programming languages like FORTRAN and COBOL.

A turning point in computer science has been the age of artificial intelligence (AI). With the development of machine learning and neural networks in the 1950s and 1960s, Alan Turing's original idea for artificial intelligence (AI) gained traction. But until the late 20th century, when processing power and data availability skyrocketed, development in AI remained sluggish. This sparked innovations like Deep Blue's victory over chess champion Garry Kasparov and the rebirth of neural networks as deep learning. Today, artificial intelligence (AI) affects many facets of our life, from virtual assistants to driverless cars, revolutionizing industries and posing moral dilemmas.

The birth of the internet and computer science occurred at the same time, resulting in a synergy that advanced both disciplines. The foundation for worldwide connection was built in the 1960s with the creation of ARPANET, the forerunner of the internet. The internet transformed information access, trade, and communication, creating new opportunities for creativity and cooperation. It sparked Tim Berners-Lee's invention of the World Wide

Web and the growth of online platforms, which altered sectors including media, entertainment, and e-commerce.

The emergence of massive data in the digital era has spawned the discipline of data science, which primarily draws on the ideas and methods of computer science. Traditional techniques of data analysis proved unsuitable as data quantities exploded. To glean useful insights from big datasets, computer scientists created new algorithms, machine learning strategies, and data processing systems. By allowing for evidence-based decision-making and predictive modeling, the combination of computer science and data science has changed industries including healthcare, banking, and marketing.

The field of computer science has significantly changed how people live, work, and interact. Computer science education is now crucial for educating pupils for the digital era. Education is now easier to obtain and more individualized because to the growth of online learning platforms and educational technologies. Medical imaging, genetics, and drug development have all been transformed by computer science in the field of healthcare, improving diagnosis and therapy. In the field of transportation, computer science has made it possible to create autonomous cars that maximize both efficiency and safety. Additionally, the study of computers has influenced social connections, communication, and entertainment via the use of platforms like social media, streaming services, and virtual reality.

There have been difficulties along with the growth of computer science. Data privacy, cybersecurity, and the effects of automation on the labor market have become urgent concerns. Biases and moral quandaries have surfaced as algorithms and AI systems grow more prevalent, necessitating careful thought and regulation. To guarantee that technology continues to advance mankind, the sector must take proactive measures to solve these issues.

Unimaginable changes have been made to the contemporary world as a result of the growth of computer technology. Computer science has completely transformed a number of industries, from healthcare and education to communication and entertainment, from the earliest days of computing devices to the age of artificial intelligence and big data. To ensure that computer science continues to be a driver for good development and human well-being as we go ahead, it is critical to address the difficulties and ethical issues posed by this fast growth.

3.1 Importance of computer science

It is impossible to exaggerate the value of computer science in the modern world. Various facets of human existence have been revolutionized by computer science, including business practices, communication, technical breakthroughs, and scientific discoveries. In this age of rapid technological advancement, computer science is essential in determining how society and economies throughout the globe will grow in the future.

In the sphere of innovation and technology, computer science is one of the most important subjects. New technologies are created and current ones are enhanced via the study of computers, resulting in ground-breaking discoveries and creations. Computer science is at the heart of several cutting-edge technologies, including blockchain, virtual reality, and machine learning. Industry sectors including healthcare, banking, transportation, and entertainment will be significantly affected by these developments, which will increase their effectiveness, accessibility, and dependability.

In addition, computer technology has changed how we exchange information and interact. The invention of computer science, the internet, has transformed worldwide connectedness and provided a forum for immediate communication and teamwork. We are now able to communicate with individuals from all over the globe thanks to social media platforms, online messaging services, and video conferencing capabilities. In order to protect the confidentiality and security of our online communications, computer science has also led to the creation of secure communication methods and encryption algorithms.

Computer science has grown to be essential to scientific research. Computational techniques are now crucial for data analysis, modeling, and simulation due to the complexity of scientific problems and the enormous amount of data produced. Computer science is used by researchers in many disciplines, including biology, physics, chemistry, and astronomy, to analyse enormous information, perform simulations, and derive valuable insights. The capacity to quickly collect and analyze enormous volumes of data has sped up scientific progress and created new opportunities for innovations across a range of fields.

Additionally, computer science has had a significant influence on teaching and learning. Traditional teaching techniques have changed as a result of the incorporation of technology into the classroom, making learning more dynamic, interesting, and accessible. Students who study computer science have access to a wealth of information, may work on projects with their classmates, and can participate in engaging learning activities. Additionally, the study of computer science has come to be recognized as a necessary skill set for the twenty-first century. Employers from a variety of sectors are becoming more and more interested in candidates with programming and computational thinking skills because they help people think critically, solve complex problems, and adapt to a rapidly evolving technological environment.

Computer science is becoming a major driver of efficiency and innovation in business and industry. Computer systems and software programs are used by businesses of all sizes to automate procedures, streamline operations, and boost productivity. Computer science is essential for helping organizations to remain competitive in the current digital era, from customer relationship management and inventory management to supply chain efficiency and data analytics. Furthermore, the way products and services are purchased and sold has been transformed by e-commerce platforms and online marketplaces, opening up new business options.

Computer science's contribution to solving social problems is another essential component. Solutions for urgent problems like climate change, healthcare inequities, and cybersecurity concerns are being pioneered by computer scientists. They create algorithms to evaluate medical data for diagnosis and treatment, utilize computer models to simulate and forecast climate trends, and create secure systems to defend key infrastructure from cyberattacks. Computer science offers the frameworks and skills required to take on challenging issues and come up with novel answers that may benefit society as a whole.

It is impossible to exaggerate the value of computer science in the modern world. It is the impetus behind advancements in innovation, communication, science, education, business, and society. Industry transformations, scientific advances, improved communication, and new opportunities for human growth have all been made possible by computer technology. People with a solid background in computer science will be well-equipped to navigate and succeed in the digital era as technology continues to advance at an unprecedented rate. Computer science will play an ever more vital role in creating the future.

3.2 Key concepts in computer science relevant to political campaigns

Computer science is becoming an essential part of political campaigns all around the globe in the digital age. Political parties and politicians increasingly depend on diverse computer science ideas and techniques as they try to connect with voters, rally support, and shape public opinion. With an emphasis on their relevance and influence on contemporary political processes, this article examines the major computer science principles that are pertinent to political campaigns.

In order to better understand their supporters and target certain voter groups, parties and politicians might use data analytics in political campaigns. Campaign teams may learn about trends, voter preferences, and demographic data via data collecting and analysis. They may create prediction models to find possible backers and manage resources efficiently by using machine learning techniques. This strategy aids in campaign strategy optimization, message customization, and delivery of tailored information, eventually increasing outreach and effect.

The emergence of social media platforms has changed political campaigns and given politicians access to previously unheard-of participation and communication possibilities. Campaign teams can analyze social media data, find key individuals, and monitor sentiment toward candidates and policies thanks to computer science principles like social network analysis and natural language processing. This data aids in controlling online reputation, facilitating message transmission, and guiding strategic choices. Utilizing social media effectively may result in viral campaigns, improved exposure, and the activation of online communities.

With the advent of big data, political campaigns have undergone a revolutionary change thanks to easy access to a wealth of data from several sources. These data may be processed and analyzed by machine learning algorithms to provide useful insights, forecast voter behavior, and guide campaign tactics. For instance, candidates may better grasp public attitude and adjust their responses by doing sentiment analyses of news items, social media postings, and opinion surveys. Machine learning algorithms may also be used to predict election outcomes, maximize fundraising efforts, and pinpoint possible swing votes.

Securing the confidentiality and privacy of sensitive information is crucial as computer science tools are increasingly used into political campaigns. To prevent illegal access and manipulation of voter data, campaign plans, and communication channels, campaigns must have strong cybersecurity protections. Information about campaigns is kept secret and intact because to ideas like encryption, secure communication protocols, and authentication systems. In addition, maintaining credibility and public confidence requires compliance with ethical norms and data protection laws.

Concepts from computer science make customized advertising and microtargeting possible, enabling campaigns to target certain voter demographics with specialized messaging. Data analytics may be used by campaigns to determine voter preferences and interests and provide tailored adverts that appeal to specific people. With the extensive targeting options offered by internet platforms, campaigns may target audiences based on their demographics, geography, hobbies, and online activity. Delivering customized messaging to receptive people improves the efficiency and efficacy of campaign expenditure using this strategy.

Predictive modeling and simulation methods may be used in political campaigns thanks to computer science. Campaigns may use models to predict election results, simulate policy effect, and assess campaign strategy by including historical data, demographics, and socioeconomic variables. Candidates may use these models to analyze the strength of their platforms, hone their policy stances, and comprehend the possible effects of various policy options. Campaigns may make data-driven choices and maximize their efforts for the most effect with the help of predictive modeling and simulation.

The study of computers has become a crucial instrument in contemporary political campaigns. Data analytics, social media analysis, big data, machine learning, security, targeted advertising, and predictive modeling are some of the themes covered in this article that provide campaigns with useful information, improve strategic decision-making, and allow individualized voter involvement. Political campaigns must adapt and use these ideas as technology develops in order to successfully navigate the changing environment and engage voters. The ethical and appropriate use of computer technology in political campaigns is essential to upholding the public's confidence, safeguarding personal information, and guaranteeing the legitimacy of democratic processes.

3.3 Introduction to data analysis, algorithms, and machine learning

Machine learning, data analysis, and other contemporary technological advancements are essential to many industries, including business, finance, healthcare, and engineering. This primer's goal is to provide readers a thorough introduction to these ideas by examining their core ideas, practical uses, and interactions with one another.

Data analysis is the procedure of scrutinizing, purifying, converting, and modeling data in order to derive conclusions and extract relevant information. To find patterns, trends, and insights that may help guide informed decision-making, it includes employing a variety of statistical and computational tools. A broad variety of techniques are included in data analysis, such as hypothesis testing, data visualization, descriptive statistics, and predictive modeling.

In descriptive statistics, data is summarized and interpreted to reveal more about its properties. Common metrics used to characterize data distributions include mean, median, and standard deviation. Charts, graphs, and heatmaps are examples of data visualization tools that make it easier to communicate and explore data trends visually. Researchers may assess the importance of links or discrepancies in data using hypothesis testing and sample observations. Using past data, predictive modeling creates mathematical models that may foretell or foresee future occurrences.

Algorithms are detailed instructions or processes for completing a certain job or addressing a particular issue. Algorithms are created to process data quickly and accurately in the context of data analysis and machine learning. They provide a methodical framework for converting unprocessed data into useful insights or forecasts.

Based on their use and other qualities, algorithms may be categorized into a number of different groups. Data items are arranged in a certain order using sorting algorithms like bubble sort and merge sort. Binary search is one of several search algorithms that find a target value inside a dataset. To get the best results, optimization procedures such as gradient descent repeatedly improve a solution. Algorithms that use machine learning learn from data to execute tasks or generate predictions without explicit programming will be covered in greater depth later.

When choosing an algorithm, efficiency and accuracy are crucial factors to take into account. The term "computational complexity" refers to how much time and computing power are needed to process data. While certain algorithms are better suited for small-scale or offline analysis, others are better suited for large-scale datasets or real-time processing.

A branch of artificial intelligence (AI) called machine learning focuses on creating algorithms that can automatically learn from data and become better over time without explicit programming. As opposed to being expressly programmed for certain tasks, it allows computers to learn patterns and make predictions or take actions based on data.

Models are trained using labeled data in supervised learning, a popular kind of machine learning. The algorithm picks up new patterns from input-output pairs and applies them generally to forecast the behavior of fresh, unobserved data. The two main activities in supervised learning are classification and regression. Regression makes predictions about continuous numerical values, while classification assigns data examples to predetermined groups or classes.

Contrarily, in unsupervised learning, the algorithm searches for hidden patterns or structures in unlabeled data. Unsupervised learning tasks that group comparable data points together based on their attributes are known as clustering. By focusing on the most important elements, dimensionality reduction methods, such principal component analysis (PCA), make complex high-dimensional data easier to understand.

Another subfield of machine learning called reinforcement learning is concerned with teaching agents how to interact with their surroundings and choose the best course of action based on feedback or incentives. It may be used in autonomous systems, robotics, and video games.

Data capture, data preprocessing, feature engineering, model selection, model training, model assessment, and deployment are typical phases in the workflow for data analysis and machine learning.

The process of acquiring data include gathering or getting access to pertinent information from numerous sources, including databases, APIs, and web scraping. Data preparation entails preparing the data for analysis by cleaning, manipulating, and integrating it. This might include data normalization, managing missing numbers, or outlier removal.

The goal of feature engineering is to choose or develop useful features that capture the data necessary for the job at hand. Designing features that improve the model's prediction ability calls for subject expertise and ingenuity.

Model selection entails picking the best method or model architecture depending on the features of the issue and the data. The kind of data (continuous, categorical, or text), the size of the dataset, and the goal (classification, regression, or clustering) all have an impact on this choice.

After the model is chosen, a labeled dataset must be used to train it. The model adapts its parameters or weights to minimize the prediction error after learning from the input-output pairings. The model is repeatedly updated throughout the training phase using optimization methods depending on the detected errors.

The performance of the trained model is evaluated using evaluation criteria unique to the job. For classification tasks, common measures include accuracy, precision, recall, and F1-score; for regression tasks, common metrics include mean squared error or R-squared.

Once a model is suitable, it may be used to fresh, unexplored data to generate predictions or carry out the required job. This can include incorporating the model into a program or system that can make use of its features.

Applications of machine learning, algorithms, and data analysis:

Numerous sectors have been transformed by data analysis, algorithms, and machine learning, which also has a broad variety of applications:

a. Business and Finance: Business and finance, in particular, may use data analysis and machine learning to better understand consumer behaviour, improve marketing plans, spot fraud, and make data-driven choices. Algorithms are used by financial firms for stock price forecasting, portfolio optimization, and credit rating.

b. Healthcare: Machine learning and data analysis have the potential to improve medical image analysis, customized medicine, illness diagnosis, and medication development. Predictive models may help in the early diagnosis of illnesses, identify people who are at risk, and suggest treatment strategies.

c. Engineering and Manufacturing: Supply chain management, process optimization, quality assurance, and predictive maintenance all heavily rely on algorithms. Machine learning methods aid in enhancing product design, finding irregularities in production procedures, and allocating resources efficiently.

d. Natural Language Processing (NLP): To process and comprehend human language, NLP combines data analysis and machine learning. Applications include text summarization, chatbots, sentiment analysis, and language translation.

e. Image and Speech Recognition: Image recognition applications including object identification, face recognition, and autonomous driving require machine learning techniques. Voice assistants, voice-controlled devices, and transcription services are made possible by speech recognition technology.

Machine learning, algorithms, and data analysis are critical facets of today's technological environment. Understanding and gleaning valuable insights from data are based on data analysis. The fundamental units of effective data processing and analysis are algorithms. Computers can learn from data and complete tasks or make predictions without explicit programming thanks to machine learning.

In a data-driven world, it is becoming more crucial to understand the fundamentals and practical applications of data analysis, algorithms, and machine learning. These methods and technologies have the capacity to stimulate invention, enhance judgment, and provide insightful information in a variety of fields. Exploration and understanding of these ideas will lead to new possibilities and difficulties in harnessing the power of data as technology develops.

Chapter 4

4. Introduction

Data has become a potent instrument in today's technologically advanced world that may reshape political environments, affect voter behavior, and provide political campaigns a major edge. In order to acquire insights into voter preferences, target certain groups, and create appealing political messaging, massive volumes of data must be strategically collected, analysed, and used. This is known as "harnessing data for political advantage." The power, ramifications, and ethical issues of using data for political gain are all covered in this article.

Data has completely changed the political scene by giving campaigns access to voter data like never before. As social media platforms, online activities, and digital communication grow in popularity, people leave behind sizable digital traces. When this information is efficiently gathered and evaluated, political players may better understand voter opinion, pinpoint important concerns, and adjust their message to appeal to certain groups. Additionally, campaigns may target swing voters, distribute resources wisely, and fine-tune their tactics for optimum effect thanks to data-driven analytics and predictive modeling.

Data collecting is the first step in using data for political benefit. Political campaigns use a variety of techniques to compile data on voters' political views, demographics, and voting history, including social media monitoring, polls, and voter registration records. The obtained data is then analyzed to provide valuable insights using cutting-edge data analytics methods like machine learning and natural language processing. With the aid of these analytics, campaigns may spot trends, categorize people, and develop targeted messages that have a strong impact on public opinion.

The use of tailored advertising and microtargeting in political campaigns is one of the main uses of data. Campaigns may target highly individualized messaging to certain voter groups by using data about people's interests, internet activity, and affiliations. With the use of this strategy, political actors may interact with people more personally while also addressing their issues and gaining support. However, customized advertising raises privacy, manipulation, and the possibility of echo chambers, when people are only exposed to material that supports their own ideas, problems.

Campaigns may improve voter mobilization efforts and hone their overall campaign plans by using data to their benefit. Campaigns can pinpoint possible swing votes, the undecided, and populations with low turnout using data analysis. They may use this information to strategically allocate resources, put outreach activities first, and modify campaign messaging to appeal to certain voter groups. Additionally, ground operations, volunteer recruitment, and get-out-the-vote campaigns may all benefit from data-driven analytics, which can eventually increase voter turnout in favor of a certain candidate or party.

While using data for political gain has great promise, there are also important ethical issues to consider. The worry about permission and data privacy is one. People may not always be aware of how their data is being utilized for political objectives since it is acquired from many sources, including social media sites. To overcome these issues and safeguard people's privacy, transparent data gathering procedures, informed permission, and strong data protection rules are required.

The possibility for data tampering and false information is yet another ethical problem. Political campaigns using data have the power to influence public opinion by individually targeting people with relevant messaging. This may undermine the democratic ideal of an educated and varied public dialogue by fostering echo chambers and reinforcing preexisting prejudices. To avoid the misuse of data and guarantee that political campaigns do not participate in dishonest tactics or the spread of misleading information, policymakers and regulatory organizations must adopt rules and transparency measures.

Modern politics now revolves on the use of data for political gain. Campaigns may use data-driven techniques to better understand and connect with voters, maximizing the effect of their messaging and resources. The influence of data in politics, however, also prompts important moral questions. Maintaining the integrity of democratic processes requires balancing the advantages of data use with worries about privacy, consent, manipulation, and false information. Policymakers and political actors may utilize the power of data while protecting democratic ideals in the digital age by creating clear norms, increasing openness, and advocating ethical data activities.

4.1 Utilizing big data in political campaigns

Data has become a vital resource for businesses in many industries, including politics, in the digital era. Big data has enormous promise for political campaigns because of its volume, velocity, and diversity. Political actors may acquire important insights into voter behavior, preferences, and attitudes by using and analyzing massive databases. This article investigates the role of big data in political campaigns by looking at its uses, advantages, difficulties, and ethical issues.

In political campaigns, big data refers to the gathering and combining of enormous volumes of information from many sources. Public documents, social media sites, internet polls, and voter registration databases all fall under this category. Campaign teams may analyse and combine this data using sophisticated data analytics tools, building detailed profiles of individual voters and demographic groups.

Campaigns may use microtargeting techniques and create precise voter profiles thanks to big data. Political actors may modify their statements and policies to appeal to certain voter groups by examining demographic, socioeconomic, and psychographic data. This tailored strategy increases voter turnout, mobilization, and chance of success.

Political campaigns benefit from predictive modeling made possible by big data analytics. Campaigns can predict voter behavior, spot patterns, and allocate resources efficiently by studying historical data, such as prior election outcomes, public opinion surveys, and economic indicators. Additionally, swing voter identification, resource allocation, and campaign strategy optimization are all made possible by predictive analytics.

Big data enables campaigns to accurately tailor their messaging to certain voter groupings. Political actors may increase the impact of their message and raise voter participation by adjusting their communication techniques depending on voter preferences, concerns, and demographics.

Big data enables campaigns to track down possible backers, unsure voters, and those who may not vote. By using this data, campaigns may use focused outreach strategies to organize and influence voters, such as customised emails, door-to-door canvassing, and digital adverts. Increased voter participation and campaign support may result from this focused strategy.

Campaigns may improve their resource allocation with the use of big data analytics. Campaigns may effectively spend their people and financial resources by determining the most potential regions, demographics, and topics. Campaigns that use this data-driven strategy make better judgments, spend less money unnecessarily, and get the most out of their efforts.

Campaigns may get immediate feedback on their message and tactics thanks to big data. Campaigns may assess public opinion and modify their strategies as necessary by using social media monitoring, sentiment analysis, and online engagement analytics. The responsiveness and agility in the face of shifting political environments are improved by this repeated feedback loop.

Big data's use in political campaigns raises questions about data security and privacy. Large-scale data gathering, storage, and analysis need for strong security measures to prevent abuse and illegal access. To keep the public's confidence, campaigns must emphasize data protection procedures and adhere to relevant rules.

Big data analytics algorithms may reinforce prejudices and inequalities. The resultant insights and targeting tactics may unintentionally perpetuate systemic biases, such as racial or socioeconomic inequality, if they are present in the underlying data. Campaigns must work to make their data-driven decision-making procedures fair, open, and accountable.

Big data may be used to propagate false information and sway voter attitudes. Campaigns must uphold moral standards and avoid from misleading or deceiving voters with statistics. Promoting accuracy, integrity, and openness in the information-dissemination process is a crucial component of responsible data utilization.

To protect democratic processes in the context of the rapidly changing big data ecosystem, suitable regulatory and legal frameworks are required. Campaigns must straddle ethical standards and regulatory obligations relating to data collecting, use, and storage. To combat misuse and safeguard the integrity of political campaigns, governments should also adopt explicit restrictions.

Big data has the potential to significantly improve targeting, messaging, mobilization, and resource allocation in political campaigns. Campaigns may learn important information about voter behavior, preferences, and attitude by using data analytics. To guarantee ethical and transparent use of big data in political campaigns, however, issues including data privacy, algorithmic bias, voter manipulation, and legal frameworks must be addressed. In order to fully realize the promise of big data for bringing about meaningful political change, it is essential to strike the correct balance between data-driven decision-making and safeguarding democratic norms.

4.2 Collection and analysis of voter data

Voter data collecting and analysis are now essential elements of all contemporary democracies globally. In order to get insights into election behavior, this method entails collecting data on voters, including demographics, voting habits, and preferences. Political parties, candidates, and policymakers may make better choices, create focused campaign tactics, and create policies that are in line with the desires of the voters by understanding the dynamics of voter preferences. However, issues with privacy, data security, and the potential for abuse are also raised by the gathering and analysis of voter data. The relevance, procedures, difficulties, and ethical issues related to the gathering and examination of voter data are explored in this article.

The gathering and analysis of voter data is essential for advancing democracy. Political actors may better understand the needs, interests, and issues of their people by conducting comprehensive voter data collection. Candidates and parties may better target their campaign messaging, pinpoint important topics, and interact with certain voter groups thanks to this intelligence. Additionally, voter data research may help in forecasting election results, discovering swing voters, and effectively allocating campaign resources. As a result, the gathering and analysis of voter data promote a political environment that is more knowledgeable and responsive, strengthening the democratic process.

There are several old and contemporary techniques that may be used to gather voter data. Traditional techniques include telephone interviews, door-to-door surveys, and registration forms printed on paper. Although time- and resource-consuming, these approaches provide insightful information on the traits and viewpoints of voters. Recent technical developments have made it easier to acquire voter data digitally. Political campaigns may reach a bigger audience and collect data via online surveys, registration portals, and targeted marketing thanks to internet platforms, social media, and mobile apps. Additionally, extensive demographic data that may be analyzed is included in voter registration databases that are kept by election officials.

Despite the fact that the gathering and analysis of voter data has many benefits, there are still certain issues that need to be resolved. Making sure data is reliable and accurate is a major task. Ineffective decision-making and faulty analysis might result from obsolete or inaccurate data. Moreover, while gathering private voter data, issues of privacy emerge. To safeguard people's privacy rights and stop unlawful access or exploitation, personal data must be protected. The digital divide also presents a problem since it may prevent certain demographic groups from accessing digital platforms, which might distort or impoverish data. To guarantee the appropriate and open use of voter data, ethical issues must also be taken into account.

When handling voter data, ethical and responsible behavior is essential. Voters should be notified of the collection, storage, and use of their data because transparency is crucial. Prior to gathering any personally identifiable information, consent should be acquired. To avoid security breaches and unauthorized access, strict data protection procedures must also be put in place. While preserving individual identities, anonymization methods may be used to do aggregate analysis. In addition to abiding by ethical principles, political parties, politicians, and data analysts must also refrain from discriminating actions, distorting voter mood, and other actions that threaten the democratic process.

To maintain the public's confidence in the political process, voter data must be protected at all costs. Voter data must be protected from cyber threats, hacking attempts, and data breaches by strong data security procedures. To reduce the danger of unapproved access, encryption, access restrictions, and secure storage techniques should be used. To safeguard people's right to privacy, organizations must abide by data protection laws and regulations like the General Data Protection Regulation (GDPR). Regular audits, vulnerability analyses, and employee development may improve data security procedures and reduce risks.

The gathering and analysis of voter data has completely changed how political campaigns are run and how policies are developed. Political actors may better understand their audience, communicate with voters efficiently, and solve their problems by using the insights gathered from voter data. To maintain the public's faith and confidence in the democratic process, however, ethical issues, privacy protection, and data security must be given top priority. The gathering and analysis of voter data may help to create a society that is more informed, inclusive, and democratic by finding a balance between data-driven decision-making and appropriate data management.

4.3 Microtargeting and personalized campaigning

The emergence of microtargeting and individualized campaigning in the world of politics has fundamentally changed the way politicians interact with people. Microtargeting, which is made possible by technological improvements and data analytics, enables political campaigns to focus their outreach efforts and messaging on subgroups of people based on their demographics, interests, and previous activities. The political environment has changed as a result of this individualized strategy, which gives politicians unheard-of chances to engage voters on a personal level. This article will examine the idea of microtargeting and consider how it affects contemporary political campaigns.

In essence, microtargeting is the deliberate use of data to locate and contact certain voter subgroups who are most likely to be receptive to a candidate's message. It makes use of a variety of data to build comprehensive profiles of people, such as voter registration information, consumer preferences, social media use, and online activity patterns. These profiles provide insightful information about the political preferences, interests, and issues that voters care about, allowing campaigns to modify their message, outreach methods, and placement of advertisements appropriately.

The use of data analytics and technology is at the core of microtargeting. Large volumes of data are analyzed using cutting-edge algorithms and machine learning approaches to find trends, correlations, and predictions of voter behavior. In this approach, social media platforms and online advertising networks are essential because they provide rich data sources that can be used to build detailed voter profiles. Then, campaigns may utilize this data to divide voters into several target groups, allowing them to create messaging that appeal to certain demographics or interest groups.

The use of microtargeting in political campaigns has various advantages. First, by allowing campaigns to concentrate their efforts on the most relevant and responsive groups, it improves the efficiency of campaign resources. Candidate messaging and policy suggestions may be successfully tailored to meet the primary problems and concerns of certain groups by recognizing these issues and concerns. This strategy may increase voter resonance and involvement at higher levels, which will eventually increase the chance of mobilization and support.

Second, using microtargeting enables campaigns to contact voters in a more targeted and sophisticated manner. Campaigns may use highly tailored communication techniques by comprehending the preferences, actions, and interests of specific voters. This may include anything from targeted internet advertising and social media posts to tailored direct mail and phone calls. Stronger connections between candidates and voters are fostered by such individualized strategies that evoke a feeling of connection and significance.

Thirdly, campaigns may fine-tune their message and stances on issues depending on real-time feedback thanks to microtargeting. Campaigns may evaluate the success of their messaging, pinpoint areas for improvement, and make appropriate modifications by continuously monitoring and analyzing voter reactions. Campaigns may become more responsive and adaptable via this iterative process of data-driven optimization, ensuring that their communication tactics are appealing and relevant throughout the duration of the campaign cycle.

Microtargeting has many benefits, but it also presents difficult ethical issues. The possibility for privacy violation is one major worry. Discussions on the limits of data privacy and the openness of data use have been raised by the gathering and use of personal information for political goals. Campaigns must establish open data gathering procedures, get voters' informed permission, and put strong security measures in place to protect voter data.

The possibility for furthering political divisiveness presents another difficulty. When information is only shown to those who share their values and perspectives, it may lead to echo chambers and filter bubbles. This may deepen social differences and obstruct free and honest political debate. Campaigns should make an effort to achieve a balance between tailored message and providing a wide-ranging comprehension of many viewpoints.

The way political campaigns are run has been radically changed by microtargeting and individualized advertising. Campaigns may engage voters more deeply by using data analytics and technology, and they can focus their messaging and outreach efforts on certain demographics and interests. Numerous benefits come with this strategy, such as better resource distribution, individualized communication, and immediate feedback. To guarantee the ethical and appropriate use of microtargeting in political campaigns, however, ethical issues and problems with polarization and privacy must be addressed. At the end of the day, microtargeting has enormous potential to promote more meaningful and interesting interactions between politicians and voters in the contemporary digital world.

4.4 Ethical considerations and privacy concerns

The two most important issues that come up in a variety of disciplines, including technology, healthcare, research, and data management, are ethical considerations and privacy concerns. In order to guarantee the preservation of people's rights, preserve trust, and encourage responsible actions, it is crucial to address these issues given the fast improvements in technology and the growing accessibility of personal data. The ethical issues and privacy problems around data collecting, surveillance, AI algorithms, and the use of personal data will be covered in-depth in this article, along with their ramifications and the solutions that must be found.

In the digital era, data collecting is essential for companies and organizations to obtain insights, tailor services, and enhance decision-making. However, when data is gathered without people's knowledge or permission or when it is utilized for reasons other than those for which it was originally intended, ethical issues come into play. The idea of informed consent is crucial because people have a right to know how their data will be used and should have the choice to refuse if they object. Additionally, measures for anonymization should be used to safeguard individual identities and make sure that people cannot be recognized from the data acquired. Organizations may preserve moral standards and respect for the privacy of persons by adhering to these values.

In the age of surveillance, when people's activities, conversations, and movements may be followed and seen, privacy issues are especially acute. Surveillance technology may be used by governments, businesses, and organizations to improve security, stop crime, or acquire intelligence. However, when monitoring violates people's right to privacy, it raises ethical questions since it might result in power abuses and the weakening of civil freedoms. It's critical to strike a balance between privacy and security, which calls for strong legal frameworks, control systems, and accountability procedures. To prevent these measures from being abused or utilized excessively, transparency in the deployment and usage of surveillance technology is essential.

Algorithms based on artificial intelligence (AI) are likewise fraught with ethical issues, especially when it comes to prejudice and discrimination. Decisions affecting people's life, such as those regarding employment practices, loan approvals, and criminal justice outcomes, are increasingly being made by AI systems. These algorithms, however, have the potential to reinforce and amplify existing social prejudices and provide discriminatory results if they are developed using biased or inadequate data. Fairness, accountability, and openness are required in the creation and use of AI, according to ethical principles. To reduce prejudice and advance ethical AI practices, it is essential to audit and test algorithms for bias, diversity the teams that develop them, and include stakeholders in the decision-making process.

Another topic that creates ethical questions and privacy issues is the usage of personal data. Personal information has increased in value as a result of the growth of social media, internet platforms, and data-driven advertising. When personal information is gathered and utilized without people's agreement or to influence behavior, ethical questions are raised. The Cambridge Analytica controversy is a well-known illustration of how personal information may be abused for political and economic ends, causing privacy concerns and the possible manipulation of democratic processes. By giving people control over their personal information and requiring businesses to treat it responsibly, data protection laws like the General it Protection Regulation (GDPR) aim to allay these worries.

A diversified strategy is needed to properly handle ethical issues and privacy concerns. Priority should be given to creating thorough legal frameworks and regulations that safeguard people' rights to privacy, regulate the gathering and use of data, and guarantee responsibility for any violations or improper usage. To continue to be useful and successful, these policies must adapt to the changing technology world. Organizations must also adopt responsible data practices, such as gaining informed permission, putting in place strong security measures, and being open and honest about how they use data. Techniques for data anonymization, encryption, and secure data storage may assist safeguard people's privacy and lessen the chance of unlawful access.

In order to resolve ethical issues and privacy problems, education and awareness are crucial. Information on rights, the effects of data collection and use, and privacy protection measures should be made available to people. Promoting digital literacy and encouraging a culture of ethical data usage may enable people to take charge of their own choices and hold companies accountable. In order to create best practices, exchange information, and jointly solve ethical issues and privacy concerns, stakeholders—including governments, companies, academic institutions, and civil society organizations—must work together.

Privacy issues and ethical considerations are critical in the digital age. To safeguard people's rights, maintain trust, and encourage responsible behavior, it is critical to address these issues as technology develops and personal data becomes more readily available. Privacy may be protected and ethical standards can be kept through assuring informed permission, balancing security and privacy, reducing algorithmic bias, and respecting people's sovereignty over their personal information. Society can negotiate the difficulties of the digital world while safeguarding individual rights and fostering ethical behavior via thorough legal frameworks, responsible data practices, education, and cooperation.

Chapter 5

Digital Campaigning: The Power of Pixels

5. Introduction

Digital campaigning has become a potent instrument for political, social, and economic activities in today's linked world. The use of pixels in digital campaigning has grown in importance with the quick development of technology and the ubiquitous usage of the internet. The basis for successful communication, engagement, and persuasion in the digital sphere is pixels, the components of digital imaging. This article examines the several facets of digital campaigning, emphasizing the influence of pixels on narratives, community mobilization, and public opinion.

The introduction of the internet transformed conventional campaigning strategies by providing new ways for political candidates, groups, and companies to connect with their target audiences. Simple websites and email newsletters gave way to sophisticated, data-driven plans for digital advocacy. In this progression, pixels are essential because they make it possible to create aesthetically attractive websites, arresting commercials, and interesting social media content.

A key component of effective digital marketing is visual communication. Pixels make it possible to produce and share powerful visual material, such as photos, infographics, and movies. For drawing attention, delivering messages, and eliciting emotions, high-resolution pictures and videos are crucial. These pictures can be rendered precisely thanks to pixels, resulting in clarity and detail that appeal to viewers and increase marketing efficacy.

User experience (UX) is important in digital campaigning because it affects how people engage with the contents. Pixels help to create aesthetically beautiful and approachable user interfaces that make engagement and navigation simple. The proper use of pixels guarantees a great UX, enabling visitors to investigate campaign material and conduct desired actions on anything from well-designed websites to interactive apps.

Advanced data monitoring and analytics are made possible by pixels, giving users insightful data on their preferences and activity. Digital campaigns may be tailored and targeted to certain demographics, increasing their effect, by making use of this data. Campaign managers may utilize pixels to assess user engagement, like as click-through rates and conversion rates, and to adjust their plans in response to real-time data.

With their large audiences and potential for viral marketing, social media platforms have become crucial to digital campaigns. In order to make aesthetically attractive social media posts, infographics, and videos that draw viewers' attention as they browse through their feeds, pixels are essential. Using pixels makes sure that campaign materials stand out in the sea of information, which raises the chance of shares, likes, and comments and, eventually, broadens the campaign's audience.

Influencer marketing has become more popular in the digital sphere as people utilize their online following and visibility to support politicians, causes, and goods. Influencers may use pixels to create visually appealing material that is intriguing and supports the objectives of the campaign. Influencers may increase the aesthetic appeal and trustworthiness of their content, attracting more viewers and increasing engagement, by employing pixels efficiently.

Additionally, pixels are important in online fundraising campaigns. People might be motivated to donate to a cause or campaign via attractive contribution sites and captivating graphics. Pixels make sure that the fundraising material is presentable and expert, giving prospective donors reason to believe in it. Organizations may increase their chances of generating donations and reaching their financial goals by adding pixels into fundraising mailings, social media campaigns, and website designs.

Users are given an immersive and engaging experience via gamification and interactive marketing, which deepens relationships and boosts engagement. Pixels help to provide aesthetically appealing and engaging interactive components like quizzes, competitions, and gamified experiences. These interactions draw consumers in, increase engagement, and promote social sharing, ultimately extending the reach of the campaign.

While there is no denying the power of pixels in digital campaigning, privacy concerns and ethical issues must also be taken into account. Organizations and campaign managers must emphasize user privacy and follow transparent data procedures. Maintaining confidence and legitimacy in digital marketing requires observing opt-out requests, gaining informed permission, and preserving personal information.

Pixels are becoming essential instruments for efficient campaigning in the digital era. Pixels provide campaigners the ability to grab audiences' attention, keep them engaged, and influence narratives via visually attractive material, targeted targeting, and data-driven techniques. However, it is crucial to use this power ethically while taking data privacy issues into account. Digital campaigns may inspire change, rally communities, and sway public opinion in the changing digital world by wisely and efficiently using the power of pixels.

5.1 The role of websites, social media, and mobile applications

There is no doubting the importance of websites, social media, and mobile apps in the current digital era. These electronic platforms have completely changed how we interact with the outside world, communicate, get information, and do business. Social media links individuals on a worldwide scale, websites act as online marketplaces, and mobile apps provide easy access to entertainment and services. We shall examine the significant effects of internet, social media, and mobile apps on numerous facets of our life in this article.

Websites are crucial tools for establishing an online presence for companies, organizations, and people. They operate as digital hubs that enable transactions, exhibit goods and services, and disseminate information. Websites have leveled the playing field for companies, allowing smaller organizations to compete globally with bigger multinationals. Websites have also changed how people shop by enabling them to explore and buy goods from the comfort of their homes. E-commerce has exploded, and online markets are now an essential part of our everyday life.

Websites have also democratized the exchange of information and expertise. Anyone may access a plethora of knowledge on almost any subject via online encyclopedias, news portals, blogs, and educational platforms. People now have more freedom to study, develop, and follow their interests because to accessibility. Additionally, websites have made it easier for people to collaborate across borders and exchange ideas. Online communities and forums have grown, promoting relationships and allowing the sharing of information and experiences.

Platforms like social media have revolutionized how we communicate and engage with others. These online communities, including Facebook, Twitter, Instagram, and LinkedIn, have eliminated geographical barriers by enabling users to connect with friends, family, and even complete strangers across the world. Communication has been transformed by social media, which has removed boundaries and made real-time dialogues possible. Users may now communicate their ideas, views, and creativity via text, photographs, and videos, giving birth to new forms of self-expression.

Social media has also had a significant influence on companies and marketing plans. Now, businesses can interact directly with their target market, increase brand recognition, and utilize user-generated material for marketing. Influencers on social media have become effective marketing tools because of their capacity to affect trends and customer opinion. Due to social media's power and reach, businesses now devote a large percentage of their advertising expenditures on online campaigns and influencer partnerships.

Apps, sometimes referred to as mobile applications, have become a crucial part of our everyday lives. These apps for smartphones and tablets provide a broad variety of features, including productivity tools, entertainment platforms, and fitness and health monitors. Numerous duties have been eased by mobile applications, improving the convenience and effectiveness of our lives. Mobile applications have made it easier and more convenient for us to do tasks like ordering meals, scheduling a taxi, and monitoring our personal finances.

Mobile applications have changed a variety of sectors, including gaming, media consumption, and social networking, in addition to their usefulness. A multi-billion dollar business, gaming apps draw millions of users and provide immersive experiences in a range of genres. With the advent of media streaming applications, we can now access movies, TV episodes, and music whenever we want. By enabling users to connect and participate while on the move, social networking applications have broadened the audience of social media platforms.

The popularity and importance of mobile apps have been boosted by the pervasive usage of mobile devices and the availability of internet access. These applications make use of the GPS, cameras, and other smartphone features to provide location-based services and tailored experiences. Mobile applications have transformed into indispensable companions in our daily lives, from navigation apps leading us through unknown regions to fitness apps monitoring our workout routines.

It is impossible to overestimate the importance of mobile apps, social media, and websites in the current digital world. Websites have facilitated information interchange, given corporations more influence, and changed how we study and purchase. Social media platforms have transformed communication, making it possible to interact with people across the world and changing marketing tactics. Mobile apps have revolutionized several sectors and improved our everyday lives by bringing convenience, entertainment, and productivity right at our fingertips. The significance of these platforms will probably increase as technology develops, influencing how we live, work, and engage with the outside world.

5.2 Online advertising and its impact on political campaigns

Online advertising has completely changed the way political campaigns are run, giving candidates and political parties access to a previously unheard-of number of people. Politicians may now more effectively target certain populations, magnify their messaging, and influence public opinion thanks to the growth of digital platforms and social media. This article examines how internet advertising affects political campaigns, highlighting its benefits, drawbacks, moral implications, and general consequences.

Reaching a large audience is one of the main benefits of internet advertising in political campaigns. Online platforms, in contrast to conventional forms of advertising, offer a worldwide audience, allowing politicians to interact with followers, organize volunteers, and raise money from all over the globe. Online advertising also enables precision targeting, guaranteeing that messages are sent to certain populations, increasing the likelihood that they will resonate with voters. The use of successful microtargeting, which involves modifying messages to appeal to specific voters based on their interests, demographics, and online activity, is made possible by this individualized approach.

Online advertising also has the benefit of being more affordable than conventional media outlets. Digital platforms provide adaptable advertising solutions that may be adjusted to match a variety of campaign budgets. Real-time analytics provide insightful information about the efficacy of various campaigns and enable tweaks to maximize outcomes, enabling online advertising to be adjusted for maximum impact. Additionally, internet advertising provides a wider variety of content types, including as video commercials, interactive banners, and sponsored social media posts, enabling politicians to experiment and identify the formats that are most appealing to their target audience.

Despite its benefits, political campaign advertising via the internet comes with a number of difficulties and moral dilemmas. The dissemination of false information and the possibility for targeted disinformation efforts are two problems. Politicians and political organizations may fabricate and broadcast false or misleading material to influence public opinion since they have the power to micro target certain audiences. The integrity of the election process is under jeopardy as a result, and regulatory measures are needed to guarantee accountability and openness in online political advertising.

The violation of privacy is a further problem. To offer tailored adverts, online advertising depends on gathering and analyzing consumer data. This poses issues with the exploitation of personal data and the degradation of privacy rights. Political campaigns need to find a happy medium between successful advertising strategies and privacy protection. User awareness of how their data is used for political advertising should be ensured through transparent data collection and permission methods.

Political campaigns have been significantly impacted by online advertising, which has changed the nature of dialogue between candidates and voters. It has democratized information access, enabling political outsiders and underrepresented voices to take on powerful incumbents. Digital platforms have given grassroots movements a platform, allowing them to avoid conventional media gatekeepers and directly reach a larger audience.

Online advertising has also made it easier to run real-time interaction and fast response campaigns. Politicians may use social media to swiftly react to breaking news, manage storylines, and influence public image. Political dialogue has become more rapid and intense, but this has also exacerbated polarization and the growth of echo chambers, where people only hear information that supports their own opinions.

Online advertising has a noticeable impact on fundraising initiatives as well. Online platforms may be used by political campaigns to rally followers, gather modest contributions, and foster a feeling of belonging and common purpose. Campaign finance has become more democratic thanks to crowdsourcing websites and social media campaigns, which has decreased the need for big funders and may increase the number of people who participate in politics.

Political campaigns have been transformed by online advertising, which has opened up new channels for participation, money, and communication. Because of its benefits, including its reach, targeting ability, and cost-effectiveness, politicians may now contact people in previously unheard-of ways. To guarantee openness, accountability, and moral conduct in online political advertising, problems including disinformation, privacy concerns, and the potential for divisiveness need for careful examination and legal frameworks. The integrity and fairness of political campaigns in the future will depend on finding a balance between the advantages and disadvantages of internet advertising.

5.3 The use of social media platforms for campaigning and engagement

The introduction and widespread use of social media platforms in recent years have completely changed how people engage and communicate with one another. These platforms provide distinctive chances for people and organizations to connect with a large audience and interact with them about diverse concerns. Social movements and political campaigns alike have used social media's transformational capacity to their advantage for involvement and campaigning. This article examines social media platforms' effect, difficulties, and possibilities to influence public debate on political campaigns and involvement.

The rise of social media has substantially changed how political campaigns are run. In the past, political campaigns disseminated their messages via mass media outlets like television, radio, and newspapers. However, in order to engage with people directly, political candidates today depend heavily on social media sites like Facebook,

Twitter, Instagram, and YouTube. These platforms provide interactive, real-time communication channels that let candidates connect with their base, communicate their policy stances, and organize voters.

The capacity of social media platforms to reach a wide range of consumers is one of its primary advantages for political campaigns. Social media, which has a wider geographic reach than conventional media channels, enables campaigns to reach voters everywhere. These platforms furthermore provide extensive targeting features that let campaigns target certain demographics, hobbies, and behaviors. Political campaigns may provide customized messages to various voter groups thanks to this degree of audience segmentation, boosting their effect and resonance.

Social media platforms are excellent at encouraging involvement and organizing supporters. To promote engagement and foster a feeling of community among their followers, candidates may make use of a variety of features, including likes, comments, shares, and hashtags. Additionally, social media promotes two-way contact, enabling candidates to pay attention to the issues of their supporters, answer questions, and immediately react to criticism. Social media's interactive features enable campaigns to build bonds with their supporters, cultivate loyalty, and inspire people to do activities like volunteering, giving, and grassroots organizing.

Political campaigns may use social media platforms as a potent megaphone to magnify their ideas and influence public narratives. Campaigns may grab the attention of millions of people and promote awareness by using viral content, arresting imagery, and captivating narrative. Furthermore, the interactive aspect of social media promotes user-generated material, allowing supporters to act as their own advocates by sharing posts, videos, and testimonials about the campaign. This natural dissemination of campaign messages broadens their appeal and credibility, having an influence much beyond that of conventional media outlets.

Political campaigns may benefit greatly from the real-time feedback and data insights provided by social media platforms. Candidates may listen in on social media discussions, follow sentiment analyses, and determine how the public feels about important subjects. With the use of data-driven decision-making, campaigns may better target their message and modify their strategy in response to audience feedback. Additionally, social media analytics provide thorough demographic and interaction numbers, allowing campaigns to evaluate their reach, gauge the efficiency of various strategies, and maximize their engagement efforts.

While social media platforms provide previously unheard-of chances for political involvement and campaigning, they also present difficulties and ethical dilemmas. A major worry is the proliferation of false information, fake news, and disinformation efforts. To maintain the integrity of political dialogue, social media platforms must address concerns about content filtering, fact-checking, and algorithmic bias. Concerns about privacy, data breaches, and the manipulation of user data also cast doubt on the morality of using personal data for political ends. It is still difficult to strike a balance between freedom of expression and appropriate platform administration.

Democratic processes have been significantly impacted by the usage of social media platforms for interaction and campaigning. On the one hand, technology has strengthened underrepresented voices, supported grassroots movements, and elevated previously disengaged people' political engagement. However, it has also sparked worries about echo chambers, filter bubbles, and the polarization of public thought. The deliberative character of democratic debate may be undermined by the automated selection of material, which may reinforce preexisting prejudices and restrict exposure to other viewpoints.

Social media platforms are becoming a crucial component of contemporary political strategy for involvement and campaigning. These platforms provide special benefits including increased reach, audience segmentation that is targeted, interaction tools, and real-time feedback. Misinformation, privacy, and the ethical use of data issues, however, need for continual regulation and attention. It is vital to negotiate social media's potential for political campaigns and involvement while respecting democratic norms of openness, accountability, and inclusion as it continues to develop.

5.4 Online activism and its influence on political movements

In the digital age, online activism—also referred to as digital activism or cyberactivism—has become a potent weapon for political participation and social change. Due to the growing use of social media and the internet, both people and organizations have been able to organize and magnify their voices on a worldwide level. The phenomena of internet activism and its significant impact on current political movements are examined in this article. We may better comprehend the transformational potential of online activism in influencing political discourse, inspiring group action, and promoting social change by looking at its traits, strategies, and effects.

Online activism is distinguished by its digital aspect, relying on internet-based tools and platforms to spread information, plan activities, and interact with a large audience. Online forums and specialized websites, as well as social media sites like Facebook, Twitter, and Instagram, operate as virtual venues where activists can interact, exchange ideas, and mobilize support. Online platforms' accessibility, promptness, and worldwide reach have democratized the process of political involvement by allowing people from all walks of life to take part in political dialogue and mobilization.

Online activists use a variety of strategies to spread awareness, undermine established hierarchies, and promote change. One of the most popular strategies is hashtag activism, in which a particular hashtag is used to build a group identity and promote information sharing. Global attention has been given to hashtags including #BlackLivesMatter, #MeToo, and #FridaysForFuture, which have sparked offline demonstrations and sparked discussions on systemic concerns. Another well-liked strategy used by activists to put pressure on organizations, governments, and businesses is the use of online petitions, crowdfunding campaigns, and digital boycotts. Additionally, hacktivism—the use of hacking tactics for political ends—has become a divisive strategy, with organizations like Anonymous garnering media attention for their online activities.

Online activism has been crucial in forming current political movements all around the globe. The internet has been a catalyst for uniting, mobilizing, and amplifying the voices of oppressed communities, from the Arab Spring to the Occupy Wall Street movement. Social media platforms have transformed into online gathering places for activists to exchange experiences, rally support, and overthrow authoritarian governments. Online platforms have also made it possible for previously alone people to connect with others who share their political ideals and build groups. Online activism has enabled the global interchange of ideas and techniques, creating solidarity and cooperation among activists all over the globe by bringing people together beyond geographical borders.

Online activism has many chances for political change, but it also has many drawbacks and restrictions. The digital gap, or uneven access to digital technology and internet connection, is one problem. Individuals without dependable internet connection or digital literacy may be marginalized and their involvement in online activism may be hampered by unequal access. Online activists who try to provide factual information and alternative narratives have difficulties due to the proliferation of false news, disinformation, and algorithmic prejudice. Additionally, authoritarian governments may filter, monitor, and clamp down on online activity, which may restrict activists' freedom of assembly and speech in certain places.

Political debate, popular opinion, and the formulation of public policy have all been significantly impacted by online activity. Online activists have been able to change public narratives, shape media coverage, and hold public personalities and institutions responsible thanks to their capacity to quickly share information and organize vast numbers of people. For instance, the #MeToo campaign acquired a lot of popularity on social media, revealing rampant sexual harassment and assault, and inspiring reforms in society norms and legal framework. Online activism has also changed the way that power is distributed by giving underrepresented people a forum to express themselves and a place to call for justice.

Debate and criticism have also been spurred through online activity. Some claim that internet activism might lead to "slacktivism," in which people commit online acts of superficiality without really working to affect change in the real world. Critics also draw attention to the danger of echo chambers and the possibility of preexisting opinions being reinforced in online forums. Moreover, without persistent offline mobilization and coordination, the influence of online activism on policy results may be restricted. However, supporters contend that internet activism acts as a starting point for political participation, increasing awareness and motivating people to take further action.

Online activism has grown to be a powerful force in today's political movements, using the internet and social media to magnify voices, inspire group action, and bring about social change. Online activists have challenged power structures, changed public perceptions, and affected policy results by using digital technologies and a variety of strategies. However, there are obstacles to online action as well, including censorship, the digital gap, and false information. It is vital to critically evaluate how internet activism may influence future political participation and social justice movements as technology develops.

Chapter 6

Computational Propaganda and Disinformation

6. Introduction

The spread of computational propaganda and misinformation has become a serious problem for civilizations all over the globe in today's linked and digitalized environment. Technology's quick development and the emergence of social media platforms have opened up new channels for propagating false information, swaying public opinion, and shaping political narratives. In order to give a thorough examination of computational propaganda and misinformation, this article will look at their fundamental mechanics, effects on society, and possible defenses.

The systematic mass dissemination of propaganda and misinformation using algorithms, automation, and artificial intelligence (AI) technology is known as computational propaganda. To sway public opinion, influence political discourse, and undercut democratic processes, it strategically deploys material, bots, and targeted messages. Propagandists may influence people's ideas and actions by amplifying their messages, building echo chambers, and taking advantage of cognitive biases by using the power of computer tools.

Campaigns for computational propaganda include a variety of players, including state-sponsored organizations, political organisations, extremist organizations, and even evil individuals. Nation-states often use computational propaganda to alter public opinion, affect geopolitical events, and weaken other countries. These strategies are also used by non-state actors to further their objectives and gain an advantage over rivals, including political parties, interest groups, and fringe movements.

To accomplish its goals, computational propaganda makes use of a variety of strategies and methods. These include the establishment of phony social media profiles, the use of social media bots to automate the sharing of material, the use of trending algorithms to magnify certain narratives, and the organized transmission of incorrect or misleading information. Targeted advertising, microtargeting, and data analytics also play a significant part in shaping propaganda messages to certain people or groups, preying on their weaknesses and prejudices.

Exacerbating social and political division is one of computational propaganda's major effects. Propagandists widen cultural gaps, amplify echo chambers, and suppress critical thought by modifying material to support preexisting views and prejudices. This division hinders productive communication, undermines democratic processes, and decreases confidence in institutions, leaving societies more vulnerable to manipulation.

Computerized propaganda seriously jeopardizes the credibility of democratic processes and elections.

Propagandists may influence voter behavior, skew election results, and damage the credibility of political processes by spreading incorrect information, creating uncertainty, and playing on popular opinion. These strategies damage the basis of representative government and destroy public confidence in democratic institutions.

Disinformation and computational propaganda may have negative social and psychological repercussions when they are propagated. People who are exposed to erroneous or misleading information may have skewed views of reality, which may result in poor judgment and a loss of faith in generally accepted truths. Additionally, the continual barrage of misinformation and controversial material may heighten societal discontent, division, and anxiety.

Technological measures are needed to combat computational propaganda. Algorithms, machine learning, and AI may be used by social media platforms and technology firms to recognize and flag bad material, find automated accounts, and stop the spread of misinformation. Promoting critical thinking abilities, media literacy education, and digital literacy may also enable people to recognize and reject misinformation.

Frameworks for effective legislation and regulation are essential for combating computational propaganda. Governments and tech firms should work together to create clear rules and laws that hold platforms responsible for the spread of misleading information. A healthy information ecology may result from more stringent disclosure rules for political ads, more algorithm openness, and sanctions against bad actors.

Investing in media literacy courses and programs is crucial if you want to provide people the knowledge and abilities they need to successfully navigate the digital world. Societies may build resilient populations capable of spotting propaganda and misinformation by promoting critical thinking, information verification, and media literacy. To guarantee a wide audience and lasting influence, these initiatives should concentrate on schools, colleges, and neighborhood groups.

In the digital era, computational propaganda and misinformation provide a complicated and varied issue. Information may now be manipulated more easily than ever before because to the growth of technology and social media platforms. To mitigate this phenomenon and protect democratic values in the digital age, it is crucial to understand the underlying mechanisms of computational propaganda, to recognize its impact on society, and to implement a multi-pronged strategy involving technological solutions, policy and regulation, and media literacy education.

6.1 The spread of misinformation and fake news

The global spread of false information and fake news has become urgently concerning in the digital era. False narratives and misleading material may easily reach millions of people due to the fast expansion of social media platforms, the ease with which information can be shared, and the absence of fact-checking. This article explores the issue of false news and disinformation, exploring its sources, effects, and possible remedies.

Misinformation and false news are widely spread for a variety of reasons. First and foremost, there are many internet platforms that are readily available, allowing for the quick circulation of information without the need for stringent verification procedures. These platforms place a high value on participation and virality, which often amplifies sensational or deceptive information. The prevalence of echo chambers and filter bubbles on social media, as well as the inclination for people to seek for confirmation bias, all contribute to the propagation of erroneous information.

Furthermore, the deliberate production and broadcast of false information by malevolent actors represents a serious concern. These actors, who may include political strategists, state-sponsored groups, or simply those out for personal gain, prey on people's confidence and take advantage of information ecosystem weaknesses. They play on people's emotions, take advantage of prejudices already there, and craft gripping stories that appeal to certain demographics.

The effects of false information and fake news are extensive and serious. They impair democratic procedures, diminish public confidence in institutions, and exacerbate social division. Inaccurate information has the potential to influence public opinion, election results, and policy choices, often resulting in societal discontent and strife. Furthermore, the propagation of false information about health may have negative effects, affecting the health and wellbeing of the general population.

False information victims may experience personal injury such as monetary losses, reputational damage, or strained relationships. Misinformation may also widen social gaps, fostering prejudice, aggression, and other negative emotions. Additionally, it becomes more difficult to develop a common view of reality due to the decline in public confidence in media outlets and information sources, which impedes rational decision-making and productive discussion.

Fighting false news and disinformation requires a diverse strategy involving several players. False information may be found and flagged using technological solutions including enhanced algorithms, fact-checking software, and artificial intelligence. Social media sites must place a higher priority on the reliability and quality of material, enacting stronger verification procedures and open moderating guidelines.

An additional crucial component of combating disinformation is media literacy education. People may become more resistant to erroneous information by developing their critical thinking abilities and their capacity to identify trustworthy sources. Governments, civil society groups, and educational institutions should work together to include media literacy into curriculum and encourage responsible information consumption via awareness campaigns.

In addition, it is crucial to promote a responsible journalistic culture. Before publishing or disseminating material, journalists and media organizations must abide by ethical reporting standards, fact-checking, and verification. Media outlets, fact-checking agencies, and technological firms working together may help build a trustworthy information ecosystem that successfully thwarts the spread of disinformation.

The dissemination of false information and fake news presents serious problems for society everywhere. Its primary causes include confirmation bias, the exponential rise of internet platforms, and bad actors' deliberate manipulation. Consequences include social divides, hazards to public health, and erosion of democratic processes. However, we can lessen the effects of false information and develop a climate that protects the truth and encourages informed decision-making by using technical solutions, increasing media literacy, and supporting responsible journalism. In order to solve this worldwide issue and protect the integrity of information in the digital era, individual, governmental, corporate, and civil society activities must be combined.

6.2 The role of social media in amplifying disinformation

Social media platforms have become effective instruments for communication and information exchange in the digital era. Social media platforms have become crucial in influencing social discourse and swaying public opinion due to their wide user interaction and reach. However, this extensive network of connectedness has also made it easier for false information to spread quickly and be amplified, which has had negative effects on people, communities, and even international politics. In order to better understand how social media contributes to the spread of false information, this article looks at its causes, impacts on many facets of society, and possible mitigation measures.

The creation of social media has completely changed how information is created, used, and shared. Disinformation, which is defined as information that is knowingly incorrect or misleading, has always existed, but social media platforms have made it more common. The decentralized structure of social media and algorithms aimed at maximizing user interaction have facilitated the quick dissemination of false information. These platforms have made it possible for false narratives to spread like wildfire, often outpacing the effectiveness of immediate corrective action.

Disinformation on social media platforms is amplified by a number of causes. First off, the distinction between trustworthy sources and malevolent actors is blurred due to the ease with which material may be created and shared. Additionally, the automated curating of users' newsfeeds has the tendency to confirm pre-existing ideas, creating echo chambers that spread and magnify erroneous information. The development and spread of sensationalized or divisive information is encouraged by the attention economy model, which is driven by metrics like likes, shares, and comments, regardless of the reality of the content. Disinformation campaigns may flourish in this setting since it's the perfect climate for them.

Disinformation is amplified through social media, which has an influence on many facets of society. Disinformation operations' impact on elections has grown to be a significant political issue. Social media platforms are used by both local and foreign players to convey false information, sway public opinion, and foment social unrest. Disinformation has the power to sabotage democratic procedures, weaken public confidence in institutions, and polarize populations. Furthermore, incorrect information regarding treatments, vaccinations, and transmission methods during the COVID-19 epidemic caused confusion, distrust, and even fatalities. This is evidence that inaccurate information may have serious negative effects on public health.

Disinformation on social media calls for a diversified strategy including many stakeholders. Social media businesses must adopt stricter content control guidelines, increase transparency, and put truth above interaction metrics if they are to effectively battle misinformation. Filter bubbles and echo chambers may be reduced with the use of algorithmic accountability and transparency. In order to counteract worldwide misinformation efforts, governments may take a regulatory role by creating clear standards for social media platforms, boosting media literacy, and encouraging international collaboration. Additionally, people are in charge of encouraging digital literacy, fact-checking material before sharing, and critically analyzing information.

A mix of technical, governmental, and educational initiatives is required to successfully counteract the spread of misinformation. Social media networks have access to cutting-edge algorithms and artificial intelligence systems that can identify and flag potentially deceptive information. Platforms, fact-checkers, and researchers working together can more quickly identify and disprove false content. Furthermore, legal frameworks should be put in place to guarantee openness, responsibility, and control over content moderation procedures. To provide students the tools they need to make important decisions as they move through the information environment, media literacy programs should be included into school curriculum.

The spread of misinformation on social media platforms creates serious problems for all cultures. False narratives quickly proliferate and are accepted due to the ease of content generation, algorithmic biases, and the attention economy model. Disinformation has far-reaching effects on social cohesiveness, public health, and democratic processes. Social media corporations, governments, and people must all work together to improve content moderation, advance algorithmic transparency, put regulations in place, and promote media literacy in order to tackle this problem. We can only expect to reduce the harmful effects of misinformation and promote an educated and resilient society in the digital era via these coordinated efforts.

6.3 Detecting and combating computational propaganda

Social media platforms have developed into a haven for the transmission of computational propaganda, misinformation, and public opinion manipulation in the digital era. The term "computational propaganda" describes the slanting of online discourse, user deception, and public opinion via the use of automated programs, algorithms, and bots. Its effects on democracy and society cannot be understated since they erode trust, skew public debate, and jeopardize the accuracy of information. To defend information integrity and the social fabric of democracy, it is crucial to identify and counteract computational propaganda. This article examines the many methods and strategies used to identify and counteract computational propaganda.

Understanding the nature and workings of computational propaganda is essential to successfully countering it. Computational propaganda amplifies certain narratives, sows division, and sways public opinion by using algorithms, social media platforms, and artificial intelligence. Propagandists often deploy social bots, which are artificial accounts that resemble human behavior. These bots may produce and distribute material, interact with people, and provide the appearance that a certain viewpoint or ideology is supported widely. Additionally, computational propaganda makes use of social media algorithms that give priority to viral and engaging material, propagating and disseminating deceptive narratives.

Computing propaganda is a difficult undertaking that calls for a multifaceted strategy. In order to recognize and evaluate suspicious actions and propaganda efforts, several strategies and methodologies have been created. Utilizing network analysis, which looks at links and interactions between social media profiles, is one strategy. It is feasible to spot suspected bot networks or coordinated misinformation efforts by locating groups of accounts with similar behavior and traits. Large datasets may be analyzed using machine learning techniques to spot patterns suggestive of propaganda.

The textual and visual components of postings are analyzed for indications of manipulation or deceit as part of a second approach of detection called content analysis. Techniques for natural language processing may be used to spot emotive language, propaganda-related themes, or deceptive informational patterns. Similar to how fraudulent or altered material, which is often used in computational propaganda efforts, may be found using picture and video analysis. Sentiment analysis may also be used to identify changes in public opinion brought on by propaganda campaigns.

Cooperative efforts between technology corporations, politicians, civic society, and individual users are needed to combat computational propaganda. To detect and stop the distribution of propaganda material, platform algorithm improvements are a crucial tactic. Social media platforms may put policies in place to restrict the appearance of suspect accounts, hide deceptive material, and highlight trustworthy sources of information. Making choices more transparent by informing consumers of the content's trustworthiness and source might also provide them the power to do so.

By passing laws that makes propagandists responsible for their acts, legislators play a critical role in combating computational propaganda. Laws and regulations may specify legal parameters for propaganda efforts, provide guidance for the appropriate use of social media platforms, and empower law enforcement to take action against bad actors. Governments, tech firms, and civil society groups working together can make it easier to share knowledge and resources, which will help counteract computational propaganda more successfully.

Programs for media literacy and digital literacy play a crucial role in giving people the ability to analyze information critically and identify propaganda tactics. Education programs may help users spot and challenge false narratives, stimulate fact-checking, and promote ethical information sharing. It is possible to lessen the effects of computational propaganda by promoting media literacy in society.

Informational accuracy and the operation of democracies are seriously threatened by computational propaganda. Computational propaganda must be identified and countered using a multifaceted strategy that includes legislative changes, technology improvements, and individual empowerment. We can make great progress in reducing the effects of computational propaganda by using advanced detection methods, enhancing platform algorithms, passing suitable laws, and fostering media literacy. Protecting information integrity is a shared duty, and by cooperating, we can create a culture where honesty, openness, and trust are valued in the digital age.

6.4 The challenges of regulating online political discourse

Online forums have developed into crucial locations for political conversation, giving people previously unheard-of chances to share their opinions, participate in debates, and shape public perception. For legislators and regulators, however, the uncontrolled character of online political speech poses considerable difficulties. This article examines the challenges and complications of policing political conversation online in the modern day. It examines the conflict between the right to free speech and the need for responsible discourse, the dissemination of false information and propaganda, the role of algorithms, the danger of online manipulation, and the international scope of the internet. Understanding these issues is essential for creating regulatory frameworks that effectively strike a compromise between upholding democratic principles and retaining the advantages of a free and open internet.

Finding a balance between the necessity for responsible discourse and the preservation of free speech is one of the main issues of regulating political debate online. The internet has increased the potential influence and repercussions of free speech, which is a fundamental component of democratic society. The difficulty is in separating undesirable information, such as hate speech, harassment, or encouragement to violence, from acceptable political expression. To protect democratic principles without silencing legitimate political expression, regulators must manage challenging ethical and legal issues.

Regulators have a formidable problem as a result of the fast transmission of false information and disinformation made possible by the growth of social media and internet platforms. False or misleading information has the power to influence public opinion, erode institutional confidence, and skew political results. Effectively identifying and addressing the origins of false information is difficult due to the internet's decentralized structure. To address this issue, regulators must encourage media literacy, support fact-checking programs, and work with digital firms to create open content management guidelines.

Through the curation and prioritization of material based on user preferences and participation, algorithms play a crucial part in influencing the political debate that takes place online. The user experience may be improved, but echo chambers and filter bubbles are also produced, reinforcing established opinions and limiting exposure to opposing perspectives. Since algorithms are private and opaque, it is difficult to determine how they affect political discourse. This offers a tremendous regulatory issue. To encourage a more positive online political climate, regulators must look into methods to improve algorithmic transparency, enforce accountability, and promote algorithmic diversity.

The growing risk of manipulation and influence must be taken into consideration when regulating political debate online. The speed, anonymity, and connection of the internet are used maliciously by actors to disseminate misinformation, participate in astroturfing, and propagate propaganda. Regulators need to come up with methods for spotting and thwarting these deceptive tactics while yet protecting user privacy and freedom of speech. To accurately identify and reduce the influence of internet manipulation on political discourse, collaboration between governments, tech corporations, and civil society groups is crucial.

Regulating online political debate is significantly difficult due of the internet's worldwide reach. Due to the fact that the internet crosses international borders, it is difficult for regulators to enact laws that are unique to a certain state. One law may have unforeseen implications that restrict free speech elsewhere and the flow of information in one area. Due to different legal systems, cultural norms, and political complexities, harmonising regulatory procedures on a global scale is difficult. To successfully address this issue, regulators must create shared norms, participate in cross-border collaboration, and promote multi-stakeholder discourse.

Regulating political speech online is a varied and difficult task. Some of the main difficulties encountered by regulators include striking a balance between free speech and responsible discourse, battling false information and disinformation, dealing with the impact of algorithms, thwarting online manipulation, and managing the worldwide aspect of the internet. A comprehensive strategy combining legislative actions, technology advancements, media literacy campaigns, and cooperative efforts from governments, tech firms, civil society groups, and users themselves is needed to successfully address these issues. Maintaining democratic ideals while using the revolutionary power of the digital era requires striking the corrcct balance between freedom and accountability.

Chapter 7

Cybersecurity and Electoral Integrity

7. Introduction

Cybersecurity is essential for maintaining the fairness of elections all across the globe. The possibility of cyber attacks to election processes has grown significantly in importance as a result of the rising digitalization of voting systems and the increasing dependence on technology. This article examines the relationship between election integrity and cybersecurity, identifying problems, potential fixes, and the significance of protecting democratic processes online.

Democracy depends on electoral integrity to ensure free and transparent elections. Voter registration, voting, vote counting, and result reporting are all part of the election process' integrity. Election legitimacy and public confidence may both be weakened by compromises in these procedures. Cybersecurity is now recognized as a key component in preserving electoral integrity in the digital era, as information and communication technologies are essential to election administration.

Cyber attacks, which target both technological infrastructure and information distribution, represent a serious danger to election processes. Malicious actors are capable of conducting a variety of cyberattacks, including denial-of-service assaults on election websites, hacking into voter registration databases, tampering with voting equipment, and misinformation campaigns. These threats may result in the disenfranchisement of voters, the falsification of election results, or both. In order to create effective cybersecurity measures, it is crucial to understand the many forms of cyber threats.

There are various reasons why electoral systems might be vulnerable. Inadequate security measures, obsolete software, and legacy infrastructure might reveal weaknesses that bad actors can exploit. The human factor also poses concerns since election workers, voters, and authorities may unintentionally or deliberately jeopardize the system's security. A comprehensive strategy that incorporates governmental efforts, training programs, and technical advancements is needed to address these vulnerabilities.

Maintaining election integrity depends on the voting infrastructure being secure. This include safeguarding electronic ballot transmission systems, voting machines, and voter registration databases. These vital components may be protected by putting in place strong authentication procedures, encryption protocols, and intrusion detection systems. To find and fix vulnerabilities in the voting infrastructure, routine security audits, penetration testing, and adherence to best practices are crucial.

Secure information and communication routes are also essential for maintaining the integrity of election procedures. Social media platforms, websites, and communication networks may be used by malicious actors to propagate misinformation, cause confusion, or sway public opinion. Collaboration between election officials, social media platforms, and technology firms is necessary to strengthen the security of these channels and create tools and rules that can stop the dissemination of misinformation.

International collaboration is required in order to combat cyber threats to the integrity of elections. Sharing knowledge, best practices, and lessons gained may improve our capacity to recognize and counteract cyber risks as a group. International institutions, like the United Nations and regional organizations, may be very helpful in fostering collaboration and setting standards and rules for cybersecurity in election processes.

At both the institutional and individual levels, increasing cybersecurity capabilities is crucial. Election management organizations must make significant investments in a strong cybersecurity infrastructure and acquire the knowledge necessary to successfully identify and address cyber threats. Election officials, IT staff, and other relevant stakeholders should participate in training programs to learn about cybersecurity best practices and new risks. Voters may also be made aware of the importance of cybersecurity in maintaining voting integrity via public awareness initiatives.

The creation of legal and regulatory frameworks that handle new issues is necessary for effective cybersecurity in election processes. Legislation should be passed to safeguard election integrity and penalize bad actors responsible for cyberattacks. Additionally, laws should be passed to support election processes' accountability, openness, and auditability. A basis for standardizing cybersecurity measures across states may be provided through international accords and conventions.

In the digital era, cybersecurity is essential for preserving vote integrity. The techniques and complexity of cyber attacks also continue to advance along with technology. Cyber assaults must be prevented using a multifaceted strategy that incorporates organizational, technological, and policy safeguards. We can safeguard the integrity and reliability of democratic elections in the face of rising cyberthreats by addressing vulnerabilities, bolstering security measures, and encouraging international collaboration.

7.1 The vulnerability of political campaigns to cyber threats

Political campaigns have a significant impact on how democratic processes are shaped and how political leaders are chosen. However, political campaigns are highly vulnerable to cyber assaults in today's technologically sophisticated world. As hostile actors attack political campaigns more often in order to take advantage of their weaknesses and sabotage the democratic process, cybersecurity has become a crucial issue. This article examines the numerous ways in which political campaigns are susceptible to cyberthreats and what that can mean for democratic regimes.

Cyber threats include a wide variety of actions intended to jeopardize the security and integrity of computer networks and systems. These dangers may take many forms, from simple phishing scams to intricate assaults by individuals with state support. Due to the significant use of digital technologies and the sharing of sensitive information, political campaigns are especially vulnerable to cyber assaults. An overview of typical cyber dangers to political campaigns is given in this section. These dangers include phishing scams, hacking efforts, deception tactics, and social media manipulation.

Understanding the reasons for cyberattacks is essential for addressing the vulnerability of political campaigns. Political campaigns may be the target of many entities, such as nation-states, hacktivists, and criminal groups, for a variety of reasons. Nation-states may try to influence the results of elections or gather important information on political stances. Hacktivists may attack initiatives aimed at exposing alleged injustices or furthering ideological goals. Through actions like ransomware attacks or data theft, criminal groups may seek to profit. This section covers case studies of prior cyberattacks on political campaigns and dives into these motivations.

Successful cyberattacks on political campaigns may have far-reaching effects and put democratic institutions at serious danger. This section looks at the possible repercussions of cyberattacks, such as the deterioration of public confidence, interference with electoral processes, swaying of public opinion, compromise of private data, and harm to candidates' reputations. It also explores the possible effects on the legitimacy of elections and the larger democratic process, presenting actual instances to emphasize how serious these repercussions might be.

Adopting thorough cybersecurity measures is crucial to reducing the susceptibility of political campaigns to cyber assaults. This section looks at methods and best practices for improving political campaigns' cybersecurity posture. It includes topics like staff awareness and training, the implementation of strict security measures, the protection of communication lines, routine risk assessments, and the creation of incident response plans. It also emphasizes the value of campaign teams, government organizations, and cybersecurity professionals working together to proactively address new dangers.

Political campaigns' susceptibility to cyberthreats also poses important legal and policy questions. The current legal system controlling cybersecurity is examined in this part, along with any possible loopholes that need attention. It talks on how to attribute cyber occurrences, how to deal with cross-border cyber assaults, and how to strike a balance between national security and personal privacy. Additionally, it highlights the need for countries to create and implement robust cybersecurity rules and promotes global collaboration to prevent cyber attacks aimed at political campaigns.

Political campaigns will encounter fresh and developing cyberthreats as technology continues to advance. Future developments and upcoming technology are covered in this section since they may affect how politically vulnerable campaigns are. It examines the dangers that might be posed by deep fakes, blockchain, and internet of things (IoT) technology. It also emphasizes the significance of cybersecurity tactics that are adaptable enough to change along with the continually shifting threat environment.

The susceptibility of political campaigns to cyberattacks poses a serious danger to democratic regimes across the globe. To preserve election integrity and defend democratic processes, it is crucial for political campaigns, governments, and cybersecurity specialists to identify and fix this risk. Political campaigns may improve their resilience and reduce the dangers brought on by cyber threats by identifying these threats, the motivations behind assaults, the effects, and putting strong cybersecurity safeguards in place. In addition, robust legal and legislative frameworks that encourage international collaboration and best practices in cybersecurity must be developed by legislators. We can only guarantee the security and honesty of political campaigns in the digital era via these coordinated efforts.

7.2 Protecting campaign infrastructure and voter data

Modern political campaigns must be especially careful to protect their infrastructure and voter information. Political campaigns now significantly depend on technology to mobilize supporters, engage with voters, and gather important data for strategic decision-making. But this heightened dependence on technology exposes campaigns to a variety of cybersecurity risks and weaknesses. This article will examine the value of safeguarding voter data and campaign infrastructure, as well as the hazards that could be present and the precautions that can be done to reduce those risks.

The integrity of the political process is the primary justification for why safeguarding campaign infrastructure and voter information is so important. Elections are the foundation of the political system in democracies, and any irregularities may have serious repercussions. By focusing on campaign infrastructure, malicious actors like foreign governments or hackers may try to sabotage or influence the voting process. They might tamper with voter registration records, change campaign message, or even disseminate false material to deceive voters by obtaining illegal access to campaign computers or databases. Strong security measures are thus required to protect the legitimacy of the election process and preserve public confidence in the democratic process.

Additionally, to preserve the privacy of individuals, campaign infrastructure and voter data must be protected. Voters' names, addresses, contact information, and political preferences are among the voluminous amounts of personal data that political campaigns gather. For focused campaign outreach, fundraising, and voter mobilization activities, this data is often kept in databases. If this private information ends up in the wrong hands, it may be used for phishing scams or other types of identity theft. Political campaigns must safeguard the data they gather and make sure it is handled ethically and securely because individuals have a right to privacy.

Furthermore, the hazards that might result from insufficient security measures could go beyond the current campaign season. The infrastructure and data gathered throughout the election cycle may still be very valuable after the election. For instance, voter personal data may be sold to other parties for specialized marketing efforts or utilized in next political elections. In order to avoid unwanted access and exploitation, campaigns must continue to emphasize the safety of infrastructure and

Several steps may be taken to reduce the dangers, safeguard campaign infrastructure, and secure voter data. First, campaigns must to spend money on reliable cybersecurity tools and procedures. To strengthen the campaign's digital infrastructure, this entails using firewalls, intrusion detection systems, and safe data encryption methods. Regular vulnerability assessments and penetration testing may assist in spotting and preventing any systemic flaws or vulnerabilities.

The second important factor in maintaining campaign security is employee training and awareness initiatives. One of the most important flaws in any cybersecurity strategy is human mistake, like falling for phishing schemes or having weak passwords. Campaign personnel may improve their awareness of cybersecurity best practices, including identifying suspicious emails, creating strong passwords, and swiftly reporting any security breaches, by receiving thorough training.

Third, whenever it is practical, multi-factor authentication (MFA) should be used. By forcing users to provide additional credentials other than a password, such as a fingerprint or a one-of-a-kind verification code delivered to a mobile device, MFA offers an extra layer of protection. Even if credentials are stolen, the danger of unwanted access is considerably decreased.

Along with technological safeguards, cooperation with government organizations and cybersecurity professionals may strengthen the campaign's security posture. Campaigns might seek advice from cybersecurity companies with a focus on political campaigns to evaluate their vulnerabilities and put in place the necessary measures. Governmental organizations may provide direction, resources, and threat information to help campaigns defend their infrastructure and data efficiently. Examples include electoral commissions or cybersecurity task forces.

Lastly, maintaining campaign infrastructure and voter data requires accountability and openness. Campaigns should be open and honest about their methods for gathering voter data, their privacy rules, and how they utilize it. Building trust and assuring voters that their information is being managed appropriately may both be accomplished by openly disclosing these elements to the public. Campaigns should designate personnel in charge of data security and ensure compliance with relevant laws and regulations, as well as clearly define lines of responsibility within their business.

Maintaining the integrity of the election process, preserving citizen privacy, and reducing long-term threats all depend on securing campaign infrastructure and voter data. Political campaigns are more susceptible to numerous cybersecurity attacks as a result of their growing dependence on technology. Campaigns can improve their security posture and reduce the risks related to the digital environment by putting in place strong security measures, conducting staff training, using multi-factor authentication, working with cybersecurity experts, and encouraging transparency and accountability. In addition to ensuring the integrity of the election process, prioritizing the safety of campaign infrastructure and voter data is essential to preserving democratic principles and people' right to privacy.

7.3 Ensuring the integrity of elections in the digital age

Elections are only one of the many areas of our life where the digital age has profoundly changed how societies operate. There are several advantages to the growing use of technology in election processes, including increased accessibility and efficiency. However, it has also increased the threats to election integrity and presented additional difficulties. Taking extensive steps to address problems like cybersecurity, voting fraud, misinformation campaigns, and the protection of privacy and data is necessary to ensure the integrity of elections in the digital era. This article examines these issues and suggests solutions for preserving electoral integrity in the digital era.

The susceptibility of electoral infrastructure to cyber assaults is one of the main issues in the digital age. Voting systems, databases, and communication channels may be targeted by malicious actors, including foreign organisations and hackers, to jeopardize the integrity of elections. Strong cybersecurity measures must be put in place to combat this. Encryption methods, routine audits and vulnerability assessments, secure network design, and training for election officials are all included in this. Partnerships with intelligence agencies and cybersecurity professionals may also strengthen the protection against cyberattacks.

Traditional techniques of voting fraud have changed as a result of the development of digital technology. Effective identity verification methods are required to stop impersonation and fraudulent voting, ensuring the integrity of elections. Voter identification may be strengthened by using biometric authentication, such fingerprint or iris scans. A secure and unchangeable voter registration database implementation may also reduce the chance of duplicate registrations and guarantee accurate voter rolls. The integrity of the registration system should be maintained by conducting routine data cleaning and verification procedures.

Disinformation and false news have been more widely disseminated in the digital era, having a substantial influence on public opinion and election results. This problem demands a multifaceted strategy to solve. Governments, social media platforms, and civil society groups must work together to create and implement regulations that support accountability, transparency, and fact-checking in online material. To enable people to recognize and reject misinformation, it is also essential to educate the public about media literacy and critical thinking abilities.

The gathering and processing of personal data for electoral purposes has risen with the development of technology. To guarantee the accuracy of elections, voter privacy and data security must be protected. Governments should establish strict data protection regulations that control the gathering, storing, and use of voter data. The danger of data breaches may be reduced by using stringent access restrictions, encryption mechanisms, and data anonymization procedures. Other crucial components of safeguarding privacy include disclosing how data is used and getting voters' informed permission.

Independent audits should be carried out on a regular basis in order to boost public trust in the voting process. Voting system audits may check for correctness, spot inconsistencies, and spot possible weaknesses. By enabling safe and auditable vote records, the use of cutting-edge technology like blockchain may improve transparency and traceability in the election process. It is also possible to promote open-source software for voting machines and tabulation systems, allowing for public inspection and improving the process' overall integrity.

Election integrity in the digital age demands global norms to be established as well as international collaboration. Countries may cooperate together to build common frameworks for election integrity, exchange information on cyberthreats, and share best practices. International institutions like the United Nations and regional groups may be crucial in promoting communication and international collaboration. Additionally, the establishment of a free worldwide organization devoted to election integrity might provide as a forum for information sharing and aid in developing nations.

The election process has seen several improvements and problems as a result of the digital age. Election integrity involves a multifaceted strategy that includes identification verification, misinformation management, privacy protection, auditing, and fostering international collaboration. Governments may reduce risks, improve transparency, and protect the integrity of elections in the digital age by putting comprehensive safeguards into place and using technology. To maintain democratic ideals and public confidence in the election process, these methods must be successfully implemented.

7.4 Case studies of cyberattacks on political campaigns

Political campaigns now have access to a lethal weapon in the form of cyberattacks. Political parties and candidates confront serious risks from cyber attacks in a world that is becoming more and more digital. These dangers may damage their campaigns, alter public opinion, and impair democratic processes. This essay examines case studies of cyberattacks on political campaigns, dissecting the methods used, the causes of the assaults, and the effects on the targets. Policymakers, campaign strategists, and cybersecurity experts may better grasp the changing environment of cyber threats and develop successful ways to protect the integrity of political campaigns by analyzing these case studies.

The Democratic National Committee (DNC) breach that happened during the 2016 US presidential election is one of the most well-known assaults against a political campaign. Sensitive material was leaked as a consequence of the incident, which entailed Russian hackers breaking into the email systems of the Democratic National Committee. This case study demonstrates the cutting-edge strategies employed by state-sponsored actors to get illegal access, including spear-phishing and malware dissemination. In addition to jeopardizing the privacy of campaign officials, the intrusion also prompted concerns about the security of the political system and outside meddling in democratic processes.

Emmanuel Macron's campaign experienced a targeted cyberattack in 2017, during the French presidential election. The assault includes the release of private campaign emails and documents, which is thought to have been planned by the Russian hacker outfit Fancy Bear. This case study highlights the role that information warfare plays in political campaigns and the possibility of influencing public opinion by strategically disclosing private information. The Macron campaign breach also brought attention to the need of prompt incident response and the difficulties campaigns confront in successfully fending off cyber assaults.

The NotPetya ransomware assault on Ukraine in 2017 showed the potential collateral harm that may be imposed on political processes, while not expressly targeting a political campaign. Critical government and infrastructure services were interrupted by the assault, which had an impact on how well the nation could run. This case study highlights the connection between political campaigns and cybersecurity, emphasizing the need of protecting campaign infrastructure to avoid unintentional interruptions during election cycles.

The German Bundestag, the nation's parliament, was the target of a sophisticated cyberattack in 2015 that damaged the network and led to the theft of private information. The assault, which was ascribed to state-sponsored Russian hackers, provided a clear example of the consequences of cyber incursions on political institutions. This case study demonstrates the long-term effects of cyberattacks, such as the possibility of espionage, political clout, and the decline in public confidence in democratic institutions.

Targeted cyberattacks against political campaigns have occurred in a number of Latin American nations. For instance, during the 2018 election cycle in Mexico, the infrastructure supporting many presidential contenders was hacked. To access private data and conversations, the attackers used strategies including phishing and social engineering. These case studies highlight the particular difficulties emerging democracies confront in protecting their political systems, such as few resources, weak cybersecurity systems, and the frequency of misinformation campaigns.

There were suspicions of foreign meddling and influence activities using cyber methods during the Brexit vote in 2016. Although the precise scope of cyberattacks on the Brexit campaign is yet unknown, they highlighted issues over the ability for public opinion to be swayed via social media platforms and focused messaging. In order to underscore the need for openness, accountability, and regulation in online political campaigns, this case study stresses the nexus of cybersecurity, misinformation, and democratic processes.

During its election processes, hackers have often targeted Ukraine. A significant Distributed Denial of Service (DDoS) assault interrupted election-related websites and made it difficult for voters to get voter information in Ukraine during the 2014 presidential election. The fragility of election infrastructure and the potential to erode public confidence in the democratic process were emphasized by this incident. Election security measures might learn a lot from the subsequent assaults on the Ukrainian elections, which included malware infections, data breaches, and social engineering strategies.

Cyberattacks targeting political campaigns and governmental organizations have occurred in South Korea. A organization with ties to North Korea attacked the campaign of a well-known South Korean legislator in 2020, stealing data about the candidate's plans, supporters, and policy stances. This case study emphasizes the potential for intelligence collection, disruption, or coercion by state-sponsored actors as well as the geopolitical aspect of cyberattacks on political campaigns.

Numerous candidates alleged cyberattacks aimed against their campaign infrastructure in the run-up to the 2019 European Parliament elections. These assaults included anything from widespread denial-of-service attacks to phishing efforts. The case study highlights the weakness of certain politicians and the significance of cybersecurity education and awareness for all players in the political process, including grassroots campaigns and independent candidates.

Cyberattacks on political campaigns include influence operations on social media platforms in addition to technical flaws. Foreign actors have organized misinformation operations, disseminated false information, and manipulated public opinion throughout several elections across the globe, including those in the United States and Brazil. These case studies put a focus on how cybersecurity helps fight misinformation, advance digital literacy, and create educated voters.

The case studies that were previously covered provide important light on the complex nature of cyberattacks on political campaigns. A thorough approach to cybersecurity in the political sphere is necessary given the expanding threat environment, which includes everything from state-sponsored assaults to influence operations and defamation campaigns. The integrity of political campaigns and democratic processes must be safeguarded through a mix of technological defenses, incident response tools, governmental regulations, and education programs. As a result of examining these case studies, stakeholders may establish proactive measures to protect the democratic foundations upon which political campaigns are constructed. These strategies will help stakeholders better understand the developing methods and motives of cyber threat actors.

Chapter 8

AI and Automation in Political Campaigns

8. Introduction

Political campaigning has changed significantly in recent years, partly due to developments in automation and artificial intelligence (AI) technology. AI and automation technologies are being used more and more by political campaigns to improve their outreach, communication, and decision-making procedures. This article will cover the different uses, advantages, difficulties, and possible ethical issues of AI and automation in political campaigns.

Political campaigns now have access to effective tools for data analysis and targeting thanks to automation and AI. To find trends, preferences, and feelings, AI systems can scan enormous volumes of voter data, demographic information, and social media interactions. This data may be used by campaigns to develop tailored message, customize campaign tactics, and maximize budget allocation.

To communicate with voters more effectively and broadly, political campaigns use AI-powered chatbots, voice assistants, and automated messaging systems. Chatbots may replicate human-like discussions, respond to commonly requested inquiries, and offer information on policy perspectives. Campaigns may send customised messages, updates, and invites to events using automated messaging systems, improving real-time communication and increasing voter involvement.

Artificial intelligence (AI) systems can track discussions, trends, and public opinion about political candidates and topics on social media platforms. Sentiment analysis algorithms can determine if a candidate's campaign is often linked with positive or negative sentiment and assist in developing appropriate strategies. Additionally, AI can locate significant users and thought leaders on social media, enabling campaigns to more precisely focus their messaging.

Campaigns can anticipate voting trends, pinpoint swing voters, and predict results thanks to AI-driven predictive analytics algorithms. These algorithms can more accurately forecast voter behavior by looking at historical data, social media activity, and demographic data. This knowledge enables campaigns to target certain groups, modify their messaging, and wisely spend resources.

The development and deployment of campaign advertising is streamlined by AI and automation technology. Automated systems are able to target certain demographics, produce ad versions based on established templates, and optimize ad placements for optimal exposure. Additionally, campaigns may create convincing and captivating messages that are specific to certain platforms and target groups with the use of AI-powered content production tools.

The use of automation and AI in political campaigns poses ethical issues and difficulties. Priority should be given to concerns including algorithmic bias, data privacy, and the possibility of harmful AI usage. The privacy of voters must be protected, and data gathering and use must be transparent. Maintaining justice and promoting an educated electorate require addressing algorithmic biases and preventing the formation of echo chambers.

The public's view and trust may be impacted by the employment of AI and automation in political campaigns. To retain confidence, transparency in the use of automation systems and AI algorithms is essential. Voters must be informed about how AI is being used and how their data is being used by campaigns. It is crucial for the effective use of these technologies in the political sphere to establish trust via ethical AI practices.

The danger of cybersecurity risks and misinformation efforts rises as campaigns become more and more digital. By examining trends and spotting misleading narratives, AI may help in spotting and combating misinformation. Protecting AI systems from being used as a weapon or to propagate false information, however, is just as crucial. To safeguard the integrity of political campaigns, strong cybersecurity safeguards and fact-checking processes are required.

Artificial intelligence (AI) and automation technologies have the potential to transform political campaigns by maximizing voter outreach, boosting engagement, and improving decision-making processes. The use of AI and automation in politics must, however, be accompanied with ethical and responsible behavior. To preserve the integrity and credibility of political campaigns in the age of AI, it is crucial to address issues with privacy, prejudice, and misinformation. Political campaigns may efficiently connect and interact with voters by wisely using the potential of modern technologies, promoting a more informed and participative democratic process.

8.1 The emergence of artificial intelligence in campaigns

Political campaigns are not an exception to how artificial intelligence (AI) development has substantially influenced numerous sectors. The use of AI technology in campaign techniques has increased in popularity in recent years. AI provides previously unheard-of skills to examine enormous volumes of data, glean insightful conclusions, and automate decision-making procedures. The advent of artificial intelligence in political campaigns is examined in this article along with the consequences, advantages, and difficulties it poses for changing election results and campaign tactics.

The capacity of AI to handle and analyze enormous amounts of data is one of the major contributions it makes to political campaigns. To find trends, attitudes, and patterns, AI algorithms may effectively comb through massive voter datasets, social media platforms, and online forums. With the help of this data-driven strategy, campaign managers may learn a lot about the preferences, issues, and habits of voters. Campaigns may increase their reach and engagement by focusing their message, targeting, and policy ideas to appeal to certain demographics by having a detailed grasp of the population.

Analytics backed by AI enables more accurate and sophisticated voter targeting. Machine learning algorithms may be used by campaigns to divide the voters into groups depending on their characteristics (demographic, geographic, and psychographic). Campaigns may create targeted communications that speak to certain people or groups thanks to segmentation. Campaigns may build stronger relationships with voters by distributing targeted material across a variety of digital media, promoting engagement and raising the possibility that they will support them. AI-enabled micro-targeting enables campaigns to locate swing voters and concentrate resources on swaying them, possibly changing the outcome of a tightly fought election.

Election forecasting has undergone a revolution thanks to AI's predictive powers. Election results may be predicted with growing accuracy using machine learning algorithms that examine past voting trends, socioeconomic factors, and sentiment analysis. Campaign strategists may make informed decisions for resource allocation, strategic messaging, and decision-making by using AI models, which can take into consideration a broad variety of factors and make adjustments to their forecasts in real-time. Additionally, campaigns may assess public opinion on certain topics or candidates using AI-powered sentiment analysis, allowing quick answers and adaptable campaign plans.

Political campaigning has changed dramatically as a result of the emergence of social media, and AI is essential to maximizing its potential. AI algorithms are capable of analyzing social media data to determine influencers, gauge sentiment, and find new concerns or trends. With the use of this data, campaigns may find platforms with strong user interaction and send tailored advertisements to certain groups. AI can also assist in spotting and reducing the dissemination of false information, safeguarding the legitimacy of elections and democratic processes.

Artificial intelligence has prospects for automating certain campaign operations processes, boosting effectiveness, and allocating resources to more strategic activities. Natural language processing-based chatbots allow campaigns to interact with voters in real-time, respond to questions, and provide tailored information. Automated systems can manage common chores like data input, event planning, and volunteer coordinating, easing campaign operations. Additionally, AI algorithms may support campaigns in making data-driven decisions on budget allocation, messaging, and targeting by examining past campaign data, polling results, and outside influences.

The use of AI in political campaigns also presents important ethical issues and difficulties. It is necessary to address concerns about data privacy, security, and the possibility of manipulation or bias in AI systems. To sustain public confidence and defend democratic norms, the use of AI technology must be transparent and accountable. Policymakers must guarantee fair access and digital literacy since the digital gap and uneven access to AI-powered technologies may worsen already-existing inequities in political participation.

A paradigm change in political strategy has been brought about by the use of artificial intelligence in political campaigns. Data analysis, micro-targeting, predictive analytics, digital advertising, and campaign automation are all transformed by AI. Utilizing these technologies may boost voter involvement, campaign efficacy, and strategic decision-making. To guarantee the ethical and fair use of AI in political campaigns, however, ethical issues and concerns relating to privacy, security, and fairness must be carefully considered. AI's inclusion in campaigns will probably grow more prevalent as technology develops, influencing political discourse and election results in the future.

8.2 Automated campaign management and optimization

An essential component of digital marketing is automated campaign administration and optimization, which makes use of technology and algorithms to effectively manage and improve marketing campaigns. This strategy uses machine learning and artificial intelligence to produce more effective outcomes by streamlining operations and improving targeting and ROI. We will examine the essential elements and advantages of automated campaign management and optimization in this post.

The use of automated tools and software platforms is one of the key components of automated campaign management. With the help of these technologies, marketers can more efficiently complete activities like ad production, audience targeting, budget allocation, and performance monitoring. Marketers may concentrate on strategic decision-making and the creative elements of the campaigns by automating these procedures to save time and effort.

Optimizing marketing campaigns also involves a substantial amount of automation. It enables real-time data analysis and insights, allowing marketers to quickly modify campaign components based on the results of their data-driven choices. Automated systems may rapidly identify ineffective advertising or audience groups and make the required modifications to enhance campaign effectiveness by continually monitoring key performance indicators (KPIs) including click-through rates, conversions, and return on ad spend.

Audience segmentation and targeting are crucial elements of automated campaign management. Automation tools analyze user data, spot trends, and divide audiences based on different demographics, interests, and behaviors. They do this by using sophisticated algorithms and machine learning approaches. This degree of specificity allows marketers to provide communications that are highly tailored and relevant to certain target groups, improving the likelihood of engagement and conversions.

Programmatic advertising, which is the practice of purchasing and selling ad inventory using automated platforms and algorithms, is another aspect of automated campaign management. Real-time bidding (RTB) is used by programmatic advertising platforms to buy ad space on numerous websites and digital platforms, ensuring that adverts are shown to the most appropriate audience at the appropriate moment. This automated method of ad purchasing enables advertisers to get the most bang for their buck, cut down on waste, and precisely target their demographic.

The capacity to do A/B testing at scale is one of the key benefits of automated campaign management and optimization. To find the most successful variation, A/B testing entails producing many copies of a landing page or advertisement and testing them all at once. Multiple A/B tests may be managed and tracked by automated systems at once, and traffic and money can be distributed to various versions automatically depending on performance. Marketers can rapidly iterate and optimize their campaigns, aiming for greater conversion rates and better overall outcomes, thanks to our scalable method to A/B testing.

Dynamic content optimization is made possible by automated campaign management in addition to A/B testing. Marketers may dynamically tailor ad content depending on several factors, such as the user's location, device, or browsing history, with the use of machine learning algorithms. By sending customized messages that connect with each person, this degree of personalisation improves user experience and raises conversion rates.

Predictive analytics are also made available to marketers via automated campaign management and optimization. Machine learning algorithms are able to forecast future campaign success with accuracy by examining past data and patterns. These forecasts may guide marketers in choosing wisely where to spend their money, where to put their ads, and how to target potential customers, eventually optimizing the success of their campaigns.

The capacity to combine data from many sources is a crucial component of automated campaign management. Data from many marketing channels, including search engines, social media platforms, email marketing systems, and customer relationship management (CRM) software, may be gathered and consolidated by automated technologies. This complete data perspective enables marketers to monitor cross-channel attribution, obtain insights into the full customer experience, and make data-driven choices based on a thorough knowledge of campaign success.

Automated campaign management may also assist marketers in more effective resource allocation and budget optimization. Automated systems may identify high-performing channels and assign more cash to them, while cutting or eliminating expenditure on ineffective ones, by assessing the performance of various channels and campaigns in real-time. Resources are allocated according to where they will have the most effect, increasing return on investment (ROI) and reducing waste, thanks to this dynamic budget optimization.

Finally, automated campaign administration and optimization are crucial elements of contemporary digital marketing tactics. Marketers can optimize ad spend, improve targeting, and offer more effective outcomes by using technology, artificial intelligence, and machine learning. Marketers may concentrate on making strategic decisions and being creative by using automated solutions to conduct chores like ad production, audience targeting, budget allocation, and performance monitoring. Automated campaign management enables marketers to make data-driven choices, enhance campaign performance, and maximize ROI by enabling large-scale A/B testing, dynamic content optimization, the use of predictive analytics, and the integration of data from many sources.

8.3 AI-powered sentiment analysis and opinion mining

The way political dialogue is evaluated and interpreted has been completely transformed by AI-powered sentiment analysis and opinion mining. It is now feasible to acquire, analyze, and understand enormous volumes of data from many sources, including social media, news articles, and public forums, thanks to the development of powerful machine learning algorithms and natural language processing methods. We shall examine the advantages, difficulties, and possible effects of sentiment analysis and opinion mining driven by AI in politics in this article.

The technique of identifying a text's emotional tone and polarity, whether it is favorable, negative, or neutral, is known as sentiment analysis. Sentiment analysis in politics enables researchers and analysts to assess public opinion about political parties, candidates, policies, and other pertinent subjects. Sentiment analysis may be carried out on a massive scale using AI algorithms, allowing for the real-time processing of enormous volumes of data.

Monitoring voter sentiment during election campaigns is one of the main uses of sentiment analysis in politics. Sentiment analysis algorithms can spot trends, patterns, and movements in the public's opinion of various political players by examining social media postings, comments, and news stories. Political parties and candidates may use this information to better understand the concerns and expectations of the voters and adjust their campaign strategy as necessary.

On the other side, opinion mining goes beyond sentiment analysis by attempting to locate and extract subjective data from textual data, such as views, beliefs, and attitudes. Opinion mining goes deeper into the intricacies of people's perspectives, while sentiment analysis concentrates on polarity (positive, negative, neutral), enabling a more thorough grasp of public opinion.

Opinion mining in the political sphere may provide insightful information on the causes of people's attitudes and views. Policymakers may better comprehend the concerns and preferences of the electorate by using it to pinpoint the underlying causes that shape public opinion on certain topics. With the use of this information, policies that are more targeted and more in line with the needs and ambitions of the public may be created.

Politics may benefit from sentiment analysis and opinion mining enabled by AI in a number of ways. They first make it possible to process enormous volumes of data in real time. Surveys and focus groups, which are common traditional techniques for evaluating public mood, take time and often have a narrow scope. With AI, data can be gathered and analyzed rapidly and effectively from a variety of internet platforms, giving a more current and thorough insight of public opinion.

Second, AI systems provide a more precise study of emotion and opinion by recognizing minute details and contextual clues in text. They can detect irony, sarcasm, and other figurative expressions that more conventional sentiment analysis techniques would find difficult to understand. This improved comprehension of linguistic subtleties permits a more nuanced interpretation of societal emotion, producing outcomes that are more trustworthy and perceptive.

Additionally, AI-powered sentiment analysis and opinion mining may be used to find new political concerns and trends. Algorithms may find subjects that connect with the public even before they become popular by evaluating vast amounts of data from several sources. Politicians and policymakers may benefit from this early identification in order to address public concerns quickly and remain ahead of the political conversation.

Despite its advantages, sentiment analysis and opinion mining driven by AI in politics can present certain difficulties. Assuring the dependability and correctness of the analysis is one of the major issues. Context is crucial in interpreting feeling and opinion since language is complicated. AI programs may have trouble understanding linguistic nuance and correctly interpreting the meaning of certain statements. The algorithms must be continuously improved and tuned to account for the unique subtleties and traits of political debate in order to guarantee a high degree of accuracy.

The management of biases in the data and algorithms is another difficulty. A number of biases, including political polarization, echo chambers, and the existence of bots and trolls, might affect the data gathered from online platforms. The sentiment analysis findings could not correctly represent the genuine public opinion if these biases are not appropriately addressed. It is essential to create techniques that lessen prejudice and provide a fair portrayal of many points of view in the study.

Additionally, privacy and ethical issues must be taken into account when sentiment analysis and opinion mining are used in politics. The information utilized for analysis often originates from publicly accessible sources, however it is important to uphold data protection laws and respect people's right to privacy. Additionally, there are ethical concerns about accountability, transparency, and possible public opinion manipulation when sentiment analysis and opinion mining methods are used for political reasons. In order to ensure that these technologies be used responsibly in the political sphere, it is essential to develop ethical norms and principles.

There are several political ramifications of sentiment analysis and opinion mining enabled by AI. On the one hand, these methods might improve democratic processes by giving decision-makers a more precise grasp of the public's viewpoint. Governments may make sure that their choices are more representative and sensitive to the demands of the people by integrating popular opinion into policy-making.

Additionally, sentiment analysis and opinion mining may improve the accountability and transparency of political players. It is possible to determine the amount of public contentment and trust by examining popular perception of politicians and political parties. Politicians may be held responsible for their acts thanks to this knowledge, which also functions as a feedback system for democratic government.

However, there are also worries about how sentiment analysis and opinion mining may be abused and used in politics. AI algorithms are susceptible to being manipulated by anyone who want to sway public opinion. The findings of sentiment research may be skewed by methods like astroturfing, which creates phony grassroots groups to represent popular support or opposition. In order to maintain the integrity and validity of sentiment analysis results, safeguards must be in place to identify and counteract such manipulations.

AI-powered sentiment analysis and opinion mining have revolutionized the study of politics by providing insightful data on the attitudes and opinions of the general people. With the use of these methods, massive volumes of data can be processed, public views can be better understood, and tailored policies may be created. To guarantee the ethical and useful use of these technologies in politics, concerns including accuracy, prejudice, privacy, and ethical issues must be properly addressed. Sentiment analysis and opinion mining driven by AI may support inclusive and well-informed political decision-making processes when appropriate protections are in place.

8.4 Assessing the ethical implications of AI in politics

Artificial intelligence (AI) has become a game-changing technology with a broad range of uses, including in politics. AI has the ability to transform political campaigns, increase efficiency, and improve decision-making processes. But there are also substantial ethical ramifications to the growing use of AI in politics. With an emphasis on issues like privacy, prejudice, accountability, and the possibility for manipulation, this article seeks to investigate and evaluate the ethical implications of artificial intelligence in politics. We may better appreciate the difficulties and obligations involved with AI deployment in political environments by closely examining these implications.

Privacy is one of the main ethical issues concerning AI in politics. Machine learning algorithms, one kind of AI technology, depend on enormous volumes of data to provide insights and forecasts. Voter databases, social media platforms, and other sources of personal information are often used in political campaigns to target and sway voters. Concerns are raised concerning the possible exploitation of personal data, invasion of private rights, and degeneration of democratic ideals as a result. Strong laws, openness, and methods for informed permission are necessary for privacy protection in the age of AI in order to shield people from unwanted data gathering and abuse.

The problem of bias is a crucial ethical question for the use of AI in politics. The data that AI systems are taught on determines how objective they are. The AI algorithms may reinforce and exacerbate biases in decision-making if the training data includes intrinsic biases, such as racial, gender, or socioeconomic prejudices. Biased AI systems may have negative effects on politics, such as lopsided representation, discriminatory voter targeting, and biased policy suggestions. To prevent enhancing current societal inequities, it is essential to make sure that AI systems are created, taught, and audited with diversity, justice, and inclusion in mind.

Understanding the decision-making processes of AI systems may be difficult since they often function as "black boxes," especially those that use sophisticated algorithms. The lack of openness and accountability in AI systems creates questions in politics. Citizens may not be aware of the elements impacting political decision-making or policy development if AI is utilized to automate these processes.

The democratic values and the capacity of the public to examine and hold political actors responsible are threatened by this lack of openness. These issues may be addressed and ensured that political judgments remain responsible and understandable to the general public by introducing legislation that demand AI system transparency, embracing open-source principles, and developing explainable AI models.

Due to its potential for manipulation and the dissemination of false information during political campaigns, AI also poses ethical difficulties. Deepfake technology and AI-powered bots may be used to spread misleading information, sway public opinion, and compromise the fairness of elections. Deepfakes, for instance, can convincingly create audio or video recordings of political candidates, confusing the public and undermining their trust. A multifaceted strategy is needed to address this problem, including the creation of reliable detection algorithms, media literacy programs, and legislative measures to stop the improper use of AI in political settings. To reduce the dangers of manipulation and misinformation campaigns facilitated by AI, cooperation between technology corporations, politicians, and civil society is essential.

The use of AI in politics has the potential to worsen existing power disparities and generate uneven access to influence. The availability of AI technology is generally restricted to well-funded political campaigns or established parties due to the enormous financial and technical resources they often demand. This concentration of AI power in a small number of hands has the potential to exacerbate political inequality, skew the competitive landscape, and obstruct the representation of underrepresented groups. To stop the consolidation of AI power in politics, policymakers must assure equal access to AI technology, encourage public investment in AI research, and promote cooperation across many stakeholders.

It is crucial to analyze and deal with the ethical issues that develop when AI gets more and more incorporated into political processes. The main ethical issues include privacy issues, biases, accountability and transparency, misinformation and manipulation, uneven access, and power disparities. Policymakers may negotiate the complicated convergence of AI and politics in an ethically responsible way by enacting rigorous rules, fostering openness, supporting justice and diversity, and stimulating public conversation. To protect the integrity of political processes and sustain public confidence in democratic institutions, it is essential to ensure that AI technologies are in line with democratic ideals and values.

Chapter 9

Online Fundraising and Grassroots Mobilization

9. Introduction

Online fundraising and grassroots mobilization have become potent instruments for social and political movements in the current age of connection and technology. Organizing and mobilizing people at the local level is what is meant by grassroots mobilization as opposed to online fundraising, which is the practice of collecting money using digital channels. Both approaches have completely changed how groups and people interact with their followers, inspire public support, and accomplish their objectives. The ideas of internet fundraising and grassroots mobilization will be covered in depth in this article, along with their significance, tactics, and effects on different social and political movements.

Since the advent of the internet and technological improvements, online fundraising has become more popular. In comparison to conventional fundraising techniques, it has several benefits, including improved accessibility, cost-effectiveness, and the capacity to reach a worldwide audience. Organizations and individuals may efficiently and effectively launch campaigns, share inspiring tales, and collect money using internet channels.

The development of compelling and persuading tales is one of the essential components of effective internet fundraising. Fundraisers may emotionally connect with prospective contributors by using the power of narrative, inspiring people to donate to the cause. This may be accomplished by sending out customized messages, movies, and other visual materials that emphasize the importance of contributions and the urgent nature of the current problem.

Social media has also become a vital tool for internet fundraising. Numerous chances exist on websites like Facebook, Twitter, and Instagram to raise awareness, get followers, and raise money. These platforms provide fundraisers the ability to take use of the strength of networks by encouraging supporters to spread the word about the cause to their friends and family, thus increasing the campaign's potential audience.

Data-driven tactics must be used if internet fundraising is to be as successful as possible. Campaigns that are specifically tailored to their target audiences have a higher chance of success. This is accomplished through analyzing the demographics, preferences, and behavior patterns of donors. Organizations may follow the development of their campaigns and make required modifications in real-time by using fundraising systems that include sophisticated analytics and monitoring capabilities.

On the other side, grassroots mobilization focuses on gaining support and enacting change from the bottom up. It entails bringing people together at the local level and enabling them to act as a group on social, political, or environmental concerns. Grassroots movements often start with a small number of ardent people who are committed to a cause, and via successful mobilization efforts, they seek to increase their impact and reach.

Community organizing is a key tactic of grassroots mobilization. This entails interacting with regional communities, running outreach initiatives, and cultivating connections with important players. Grassroots activists seek to empower locals by giving them the instruments, materials, and information need to promote change. This may be accomplished via seminars, training sessions, and open forums where people can learn more about the problem at hand, share their experiences, and create plans of action for a group effort.

The use of conventional and digital communication channels to spread information and rally supporters is a crucial component in grassroots mobilization. Door-to-door canvassing, public speeches, online petitions, and the use of social media platforms may all be examples of this. Grassroots movements may include a variety of people, including some who might not be engaged on internet platforms, by combining offline and online approaches.

Social media has been more important for grassroots mobilization in recent years. Movements may now quickly distribute their thoughts, increase awareness, and plan demonstrations and other events thanks to platforms like Twitter, Instagram, and YouTube. By uniting people and bringing them together around a shared cause, hashtags and viral campaigns may help grassroots movements attain national or even worldwide prominence.

A variety of social and political movements throughout the globe have been significantly impacted by the union of internet financing with grassroots mobilization. These tactics have enabled people and groups to take on challenging problems, collect substantial sums of money, and make a difference in their local communities. Online fundraising and grassroots mobilization have been shown to be transformational instruments for social action, from human rights campaigns to disaster relief initiatives.

For instance, internet fundraising enables quick reaction and help during natural catastrophes or humanitarian emergencies. Through crowdfunding sites, people may give directly to impacted areas, avoiding conventional middlemen and ensuring that money gets to those in need as soon as possible. Efforts at grassroots mobilization may also organize volunteers, gather necessary supplies, and aid afflicted communities.

Online financing and grassroots organizing have also been very important in political campaigns. Candidates may use online fundraising tools to increase participation and lessen dependency on major contributors while raising money for their campaigns. Door-to-door canvassing, phone banking, and rally planning are examples of grassroots mobilization strategies that have been effective in stoking support, energizing voters, and influencing public opinion.

The worlds of internet fundraising and grassroots mobilization do, however, have difficulties. It may be tough for individual fundraisers to stand out and achieve awareness due to the overwhelming number of internet campaigns. Building reputation and trust is also important since prospective contributors need to know their money will be used wisely. Similar to this, successful community engagement and mobilization depend on consistent effort and resources. It may take time and effort to combat indifference, assemble volunteers, and oversee logistics.

The world of social and political activity has changed as a result of grassroots organizing and online financing. Utilizing technology effectively enables people and groups to organize supporters, generate finances, and raise awareness like never before. Despite the difficulties, these tactics have a huge potential for influence and change. In order to accomplish their objectives and make the world a better place, it will be critical moving ahead for activists, organizations, and political campaigns to properly use these tools, embracing new technology and interacting with supporters in creative ways.

9.1 Crowdfunding and digital fundraising platforms

Digital fundraising platforms and crowdfunding have altered how people, businesses, and organizations raise money for their endeavors, initiatives, and causes. Online platforms that link artists with prospective funders and investors have augmented, if not entirely replaced, conventional ways of fundraising in this digital age. Digital fundraising platforms provide a simplified method for obtaining contributions and supporting charity organizations, whilst crowdfunding platforms give people and companies a way to expose their ideas and campaigns to a large audience. The idea of crowdfunding, its numerous forms, and the advantages it provides will all be covered in this article. It will also examine the capabilities of online fundraising platforms and how they influence charitable activities.

Crowdfunding is the technique of obtaining donations from a large number of individuals for a project, endeavor, or cause, usually using an internet platform. It is founded on the notion of teamwork, in which people pool their resources to support causes they believe in. Platforms for crowdfunding serve as middlemen, bringing together project creators and possible investors. These platforms provide artists a place to present their work, lay out their objectives, and describe how the cash will be used. The initiatives that appeal to interested parties may subsequently get financial support from those persons, often in return for awards or early access to the finished product.

Reward-based crowdfunding is one of the most popular varieties. In this strategy, those who contribute to a project's campaigns get a variety of incentives or prizes. These benefits may include early product access, premium goods, or specialized experiences. In the reward-based crowdfunding sector, websites like Kickstarter and Indiegogo have become well-known because they enable creators to present their unique ideas and obtain cash from potential supporters.

Another prominent sort of crowdfunding that has gained popularity recently is equity crowdfunding. stock crowdfunding, as opposed to reward-based crowdfunding, enables people to put money into early-stage companies or startups in return for stock or ownership holdings. With the help of this approach, more people may access investment possibilities and become owners in profitable businesses. Platforms like Seedrs and Crowdcube have established themselves as industry leaders in equity crowdfunding by enabling investments in companies in several sectors.

There are different kinds of crowdfunding that address certain requirements in addition to reward-based and equity crowdfunding. Crowdfunding that is based on donations prioritizes collecting money for nonprofit organizations and philanthropic purposes. Donors make contributions to these initiatives without anticipating a financial reward. GoFundMe and JustGiving are two donation-based websites that have proven crucial in aiding people experiencing medical crises, disaster relief operations, and humanitarian projects.

People may now invest in real estate projects and homes thanks to the growth of real estate crowdfunding. These platforms allow investors to diversify their holdings among several properties with lower contributions. Real estate investments that were previously only available to a select few are now accessible thanks to this strategy.

On the other hand, online platforms for fundraising are mainly concerned with aiding nonprofits and philanthropic causes. These systems make it easier to collect contributions from both people and businesses, with the goal of improving the process' efficiency and transparency. They often provide resources for organizing contributions, administering campaigns, and monitoring progress toward fundraising objectives.

Comparing digital fundraising platforms to conventional ones, there are a number of benefits. They first provide a broader audience reach and access to a worldwide audience. Fundraisers may use the power of social media and digital marketing via online platforms to boost awareness of their cause and draw in new donations. The likelihood of achieving fundraising goals and making a substantial impact is increased by this worldwide reach.

Second, digital fundraising platforms make it easier for donors and fundraisers to donate by streamlining the procedure. In the past, it was common to collect contributions using manual processes like cash or cheques, which might be time-consuming and error-prone. Digital platforms, on the other hand, provide for safe online transactions, enabling contributors to make a contribution with only a few clicks. Additionally, these platforms often provide opportunities for recurring payments, enabling people to continually support charities.

The openness they provide to the fundraising process is another noteworthy benefit of digital fundraising platforms. Fundraisers may follow the development of their campaigns and comprehend the results of their efforts thanks to the several platforms that provide comprehensive analytics and reporting options. Transparency is advantageous to donors as well since it allows them to understand how their gifts are used and the impact they have.

Additionally, visual and narrative elements are often used in digital fundraising platforms to emotionally connect with contributors. They provide fundraisers a platform to communicate engrossing stories, photographs, and videos that personalize their causes and build a bond with prospective funders. This emotional connection is essential in encouraging people to give to and support the cause.

In conclusion, digital fundraising platforms and crowdsourcing have revolutionized how people, businesses, and organizations raise money and support causes. These platforms have democratized access to cash and made it possible for creative ideas to be realized via a variety of models including reward-based crowdsourcing, equity crowdfunding, and donation-based crowdfunding. Digital fundraising platforms, however, have improved transparency, sped up the contribution process, and expanded the reach of humanitarian endeavors. We can anticipate further developments in the field of digital fundraising and crowdfunding as technology continues to grow, enabling people and organizations to have a beneficial effect on the world.

9.2 Grassroots organizing through online networks

Online networks for grassroots organizing have become a potent and revolutionary force in modern society. Individuals and groups may now connect, organize, and affect change on a scale that was previously unthinkable because to the development of the internet and social media platforms. By enabling individuals from many backgrounds to come together, exchange ideas, and work together to solve social, political, and environmental concerns, this kind of organizing has democratized activism. The relevance, advantages, drawbacks, and prospective advancements of grassroots organizing using internet networks will all be discussed in this article.

Creating a movement or campaign from the bottom up with active involvement and leadership from common people rather than from existing organizations or hierarchies is known as grassroots organizing. It is founded on the conviction that significant change may be brought about by empowering and organizing local communities to take up problems that directly impact them. Traditional grassroots organizing methods included face-to-face communication, neighborhood gatherings, and neighborhood outreach. However, the development of internet communities has fundamentally changed how grassroots movements are managed.

Online communities provide a forum for people to meet others who share their interests, regardless of location. In order to exchange information, plan activities, and reach a worldwide audience, grassroots organizers now rely heavily on social media sites like Facebook, Twitter, Instagram, and YouTube. Through these networks, people may interact directly with their intended audience without going through conventional information gatekeepers like the mainstream media. Individuals who would have before felt excluded or powerless now feel empowered and in control of their own lives because to this direct access to knowledge.

Reaching a large and varied audience is one of the main advantages of grassroots organizing using internet networks. With billions of active users, social media platforms provide a sizable pool of potential supporters and allies for grassroots movements. Online networks provide activists the opportunity to interact with people from other origins, cultures, and viewpoints, promoting inclusion and diversity within movements. This inclusiveness, by uniting a diverse coalition of views and experiences, improves the overall effect of grassroots organization.

Online networks also make it easier to mobilize resources and disseminate information quickly. Organizers may share news, articles, videos, and calls to action with their networks in a few of clicks, igniting debate and motivating group action. Real-time updates and live broadcasting of events, demonstrations, and protests are also made possible through online platforms, enabling individuals to join and demonstrate their support even if they are unable to physically attend. The speed and scope at which grassroots movements may organize and react to new concerns have undergone a transformation as a result of this accessibility and immediateness.

The capacity to create and maintain long-term participation is a key benefit of grassroots organizing via internet networks. Online forums provide locations for continuing discussions, planning activities, and information exchange. As a result of this ongoing involvement, movements are better able to overcome obstacles, change their approach, and maintain momentum over time. Online communities enable the development of connections between supporters and organizers, fostering mutual support, skill-sharing, and mentoring.

Despite its numerous advantages, grassroots organizing through internet networks has particular difficulties. The problem of the digital gap and uneven access to technology is one of the main worries. Despite the fact that the internet and social media are now widely used, there are still large gaps in access and digital literacy, especially in underprivileged populations. The engagement of persons without internet access or who have difficulties accessing online places may be hampered by this digital divide. To overcome this obstacle, proactive efforts must be made to close the gap via programs like community technology centers, digital literacy courses, and collaborations with groups dedicated to digital inclusion.

The possibility for information overload and the propagation of false information provide another difficulty. Online networks may be difficult to navigate since there is so much information vying for your attention. Because of this, it may be challenging for grassroots activists to successfully communicate their message and stand out from the crowd. Furthermore, the social media's capacity for spreading misinformation and falsehoods may diminish the authority and significance of grassroots movements. Organizers must prioritize trustworthy sources, fact-check material, and create plans to combat disinformation within their networks in order to meet this challenge.

Concerns about privacy and security also surface when discussing grassroots organization via internet networks. Online services gather a lot of personal information, which raises questions about monitoring, data breaches, and possible activist targeting. Trust among grassroots movements must be maintained at all times, which requires protecting privacy and guaranteeing the security of internet networks. The use of encrypted communication channels, educating attendees about privacy issues, and promoting broader legal rights for online activists are all excellent practices that organizers should embrace.

The potential for grassroots activism through internet networks is quite promising in the future. New tools and platforms will appear as technology develops further, providing even more opportunities for interaction and teamwork. Emerging technologies, such as augmented reality and virtual reality, might, for instance, provide immersive and engaging experiences for gathering and mobilizing followers. The efficacy of grassroots organizing activities might be increased by using artificial intelligence algorithms to help detect patterns, trends, and possible allies inside internet networks.

It may also result in strong alliances and synergies when grassroots organizing and internet networks are combined with other social movements and advocacy initiatives. Collaboration between established NGOs, social justice movements, and grassroots activists may boost each other's messages, resources, and influence. Online networks provide these partnerships a place to grow, enabling movements to exchange tactics, learn from one another, and collaborate on projects for optimum impact.

Online networks have changed the activism and social change environment via grassroots organization. It has transformed the speed and scope with which collective action may be organized, empowered people, and increased the reach and variety of movements. The digital gap, information overload, and privacy concerns are just a few of the problems that need to be addressed in order to maintain the efficacy and inclusiveness of grassroots organizing. The future of grassroots organizing via internet networks has immense promise for bringing about good and revolutionary change in society due to continued technological improvements and growing movement participation.

9.3 The role of peer-to-peer campaigning and social networks

Social networks and digital communication have completely changed how individuals interact and exchange information. Peer-to-peer campaigning and the usage of social networks have become effective methods for promoting social and political change in recent years. Through an analysis of their effects on mobilization, information sharing, and community building, this article seeks to investigate the role of social networks and peer-to-peer campaigning in influencing societal change. These platforms have the ability to spark social movements, elevate underrepresented perspectives, and promote meaningful discussion among many communities by using the power of connectedness and grassroots activity.

Social networks and peer-to-peer campaigns have been successful in enlisting the support of people and groups for a common cause. These platforms remove conventional obstacles to admission and enable people to band together and support issues they care about. Users may establish or join campaigns, find volunteers, and plan offline events with only a few clicks. Bypassing conventional hierarchical systems is made possible by the simplicity and accessibility of these platforms, which promotes a feeling of action and ownership. This grassroots movement has been especially successful in encouraging underprivileged groups to speak out against systematic injustices and defend their rights.

Real-time updates and the amplification of previously underrepresented voices are made possible by social networks, which have revolutionized the way information is conveyed. Peer-to-peer campaigning makes use of this ability to spread information quickly and effectively. News, articles, films, and personal experiences may be shared by activists and groups to reach audiences throughout the world. These efforts may expose ignored viewpoints and refute popular narratives by cutting out the established gatekeepers. Additionally, social networks provide users the opportunity to participate in debates, pose questions, and further their education, promoting informed citizenship and raising awareness of important social problems.

Peer-to-peer campaigning and social media's capacity to elevate underrepresented perspectives is one of their most important achievements. People of color, LGBTQ+ people, and those from low-income backgrounds—all historically oppressed communities—have discovered a platform to express their stories and demand for change. These efforts provide these voices attention and credibility, allowing them to be heard more widely. Social networks challenge conventional preconceptions, promote empathy, and organize support for underdog causes by reinforcing these tales.

Online communities based on common values, identities, and interests have been made possible through social networks. Peer-to-peer campaigning makes use of these groups' strength to promote cooperation, support systems, and feelings of solidarity. Users may access information, exchange experiences, and connect with others who share their interests. These groups of people act as safe places where people may connect with one another, receive affirmation, and work together to make a real difference. Social networks allow disparate groups to interact by bridging geographic barriers, promoting a feeling of connection and group responsibility on a global scale.

Peer-to-peer campaigns and social networks have enormous prospects, but they also have drawbacks and restrictions. The integrity of these platforms is threatened by false information, echo chambers, and algorithmic biases. Language obstacles, accessibility problems, and digital differences might also prevent certain populations from fully engaging. The efficacy of these initiatives may also be hampered by corporate influence and internet abuse. Promoting media literacy, inclusive design, and strong policies are essential in addressing these issues in order to maintain the equity and effectiveness of these platforms.

Social networks and peer-to-peer campaigning have become effective instruments for societal change, transforming how people connect, organize, and advocate for their causes. These platforms have the ability to bring about significant social changes through promoting online communities, amplifying disadvantaged perspectives, enabling information transmission, and empowering grassroots movement. However, it is crucial to solve issues like false information, digital inequalities, and algorithmic biases in order to fully achieve their potential. Peer-to-peer campaigns and social networks may continue to mold a more inclusive, knowledgeable, and connected society with cautious navigation.

9.4 Analyzing successful online fundraising campaigns

Online fundraising has developed into a potent tool in recent years for people, NGOs, and companies to collect money for different causes. Crowdfunding has been a well-liked method of raising money with the development of social media and digital platforms. This examination explores effective online fundraising efforts by looking at their tactics, essential components, and the qualities that made them successful. Individuals and organizations may enhance their fundraising efforts and increase their chances of success by comprehending these variables.

Examining the current landscape of digital fundraising platforms is essential to understanding effective online fundraising initiatives. The development of online fundraising, its benefits over more conventional techniques, and the major websites that support such campaigns, including Kickstarter, GoFundMe, and Patreon, will all be covered in this part. The part will also emphasize the value of narrative, the influence of influencers, and the effect of social media on the success of online fundraising campaigns.

Online fundraising efforts that are successful have particular characteristics that set them apart and appeal to prospective contributors. These essential components—a engaging story, specific aims and objectives, a strong call to action, transparency, authenticity, and social proof—will all be covered in this section. Each component will be thoroughly analyzed, with examples of ads that used it to draw in and keep the attention of their target audience.

Social networking sites have completely changed how internet fundraising initiatives are carried out. We will examine the methods and approaches used to properly utilize social media in this part. It will go through how crucial it is to have a solid online presence, interact with the audience, tell stories using multimedia material, utilize hashtags effectively, and make use of user-generated content. The section will provide case studies of campaigns that amplified their fundraising efforts by using social media.

various online fundraising platforms appeal to various audiences and provide a variety of services. The tactics and best practices for certain platforms, like Kickstarter, GoFundMe, Patreon, and others, will be covered in this section. It will explore the distinctive features of each platform, such as campaign setup, reward schemes, interactions with supporters, and community development. Fundraisers may optimize their chances of success by customizing their approach by learning the specifics of each platform.

Data and analytics are crucial in the digital era for maximizing the effectiveness of online fundraising initiatives. The significance of monitoring and evaluating campaign data, including conversion rates, engagement levels, donor demographics, and referral sources, will be covered in this section. It will go in-depth on the tools and methods for data analysis that are available and how to utilize them to improve campaign plans, spot patterns, and make data-driven choices to improve fundraising results.

Successful online fundraising efforts may be analyzed to get important knowledge about their methods and tactics. People and organizations can improve their chances of running successful online fundraising campaigns by comprehending the online fundraising landscape, utilizing social media effectively, incorporating crucial campaign components, tailoring strategies to specific platforms, and utilizing data analytics. In a world where internet connection is expanding, understanding the art of digital fundraising is essential for reaching financial targets and improving society.

Chapter 10

Case Studies: Examining Noteworthy Digital Political Campaigns

10. Introduction

Modern political campaigns now include a significant amount of digital technology, altering the way politicians interact with voters and promote their ideas. This article seeks to investigate and evaluate a number of notable recent digital political initiatives that have had a substantial influence. We may learn more about the tactics used, the efficacy of digital platforms, and the ramifications for next political campaigns by looking at these case studies. The three separate case studies that will be examined in more detail in the following paragraphs will be highlighted for their creative strategies and their implications for the changing field of political campaigning.

Another fascinating case study of online political campaigning is the UK's 2016 Brexit vote. Digital channels were used by pro-Brexit activists, headed by organizations like Leave.EU and Vote Leave, to spread their message and garner support. To convince potential voters, they used data-driven tactics including tailored messaging and targeted social media advertising. Big data analytics were efficiently used in these ads to pinpoint important demographics and modify messaging appropriately. These campaigns were able to directly contact and influence voters by avoiding the conventional media's gatekeepers by using social media, in particular. The Brexit campaign's success showed how effective internet campaigns can be at upending pre-existing political narratives and reshaping political results.

The 14th congressional district of New York's 2018 Alexandria Ocasio-Cortez campaign demonstrated the effectiveness of grassroots internet organizing. Ocasio-Cortez leaned extensively on social media tools to engage with people and spark excitement despite having less funding than her rival. She created an accessible and genuine online presence via the deliberate use of Twitter and Instagram, which appealed to young, progressive voters. The campaign of Ocasio-Cortez embraced openness by giving behind-the-scenes peeks at her experiences on the campaign trail and interacting directly with her supporters online. This strategy not only helped her win, but it also generated discussions about the democratization of political campaigns, where close relationships made via internet platforms may have a significant influence.

These case studies provide crucial insights into how political campaigning has changed in the modern era. They emphasize the need for candidates to adapt and make efficient use of digital platforms in order to interact with voters, create communities, and influence public opinion. Furthermore, these campaigns show how digital platforms have the power to level the playing field by enabling underfunded candidates to take on well-funded political organizations. They also raise questions about the effect of echo chambers, the dissemination of false information, and the impact of data-driven targeting on political discourse.

Future political campaigns will definitely use cutting-edge platforms and techniques as technology develops. The use of blockchain-based platforms, virtual reality, and artificial intelligence may become more prevalent in campaign tactics. However, there will be a need for further research and discussion in the areas of ethics, privacy, and regulation of digital campaigning.

The case studies of the campaign for the Brexit vote, and Alexandria Ocasio-Cortez's 2018 campaign demonstrate how digital technologies may completely change the way political campaigns are conducted. These campaigns engaged voters, shaped public opinion, and achieved their political objectives by using social media platforms, data-driven targeting, and grassroots organization. To maintain the integrity of democratic processes, they also emphasize the necessity for responsible and moral use of new technology. Policymakers, candidates, and voters can all learn a great deal about the always changing world of digital political campaigns and how to best apply them in the future by studying and evaluating these case studies.

10.1 Obama's 2008 and 2012 digital campaigns

The use of digital platforms and technology by Barack Obama's presidential campaigns in 2008 and 2012 to engage voters, rally supporters, and generate money was innovative. These initiatives successfully used social media, data analytics, and online organizing tools to mobilize the support of the general public. The main techniques and methods used by Obama's digital teams throughout both campaigns are examined in this article, along with their effects on the political environment and the changing nature of digital campaigning in contemporary politics.

When Obama's team saw the untapped potential of social media platforms during the 2008 campaign, it marked a turning point in political communication. They used Facebook, Twitter, and YouTube deliberately to spread Obama's message, engage voters, and rally supporters. Through creative use of social media, the campaign was able to avoid conventional media gatekeepers, interact directly with voters, and create a feeling of community.

Obama's digital campaign team made use of data analytics to better comprehend and target certain voter categories. They created thorough voter profiles and customized messages for various voter categories by evaluating a massive quantity of data, including voter records, internet activity, and demographics. With the use of this data-driven strategy, the campaign was able to successfully engage supporters, maximize budget allocation, and tailor communication activities.

The 2008 campaign placed a strong emphasis on community organizing, urging supporters to take charge of it and interact actively with their networks. "My.BarackObama.com," a ground-breaking online platform that gave volunteers the ability to set up profiles, plan events, collect money, and interact with other supporters in their neighborhoods, was introduced by the campaign. The campaign's success in assembling a large coalition of supporters may be attributed to the grassroots strategy, which promoted a feeling of inclusion and engagement.

By using internet networks, Obama's digital campaign transformed fundraising. They used a range of strategies, including email solicitations, online contribution platforms, and customized fundraising appeals, to persuade a large number of individual donors to make modest gifts. The campaign's capacity to harness the strength of internet networks and viral sharing greatly increased their capacity for fundraising and offered a competitive option to conventional high-dollar contributors.

Obama's team continued to grow their social media presence in 2012 as they built on the success of their campaign in 2008. Through social media sites like Facebook, Twitter, and Instagram, they actively interacted with their followers, promoting conversation, disseminating campaign updates, and energizing grassroots initiatives. With a wider audience to target, the campaign was able to engage younger voters who were more inclined to read the news and participate in political discourse online.

Given the growing popularity of smartphones, the 2012 campaign gave mobile optimization a priority in order to reach voters on the move. They created a mobile app that offered updates on the campaign, volunteer opportunities, and resources for voter registration and mobilization to supporters. The smartphone app was an effective tool for coordination, allowing real-time communication and improving volunteer interactions with voters.

In 2012, the campaign used advanced digital advertising techniques to target certain geographic and demographic groups of voters. The campaign pinpointed crucial swing states using data analytics, then microtargeted digital advertising to appeal to those states' uncertain voters. Especially in key swing states, the campaign was able to maximize the effect of their message and optimize their advertising expenditure because to this precise targeting.

In 2012, the campaign's data analytics skills were improved further, allowing for more targeted voter communication. The campaign created a thorough voter database with data on demographics, voting behavior, and issue preferences by combining online and offline data sources. Through targeted emails, social media interaction, and door-to-door canvassing, this comprehensive information enabled individualized outreach, ensuring that supporters got messages that spoke to their particular issues.

Obama's internet operations were especially effective at energizing young people, who are often less involved in politics. The campaigns successfully tapped into the idealistic and tech-savvy nature of the millennial generation, inspiring people to give, vote, and engage actively by using social media and online organizing tools. The focus on youth participation had a long-lasting effect on political campaigns that followed, with politicians realizing the value of internet media in connecting with and motivating younger groups.

Obama's internet initiatives were so successful that they changed the rules of political campaigning and encouraged other candidates to use them. The campaigns showed the effectiveness of internet organizing tools, social media, and data analytics in swaying public opinion, rallying supporters, and generating money. Obama's teams used ground-breaking tactics that have subsequently been incorporated into many aspects of contemporary political campaigns, influencing how politicians interact with voters and spread awareness of their programs.

By using the power of digital platforms and technology to engage voters, rally supporters, and raise money, Obama's digital campaigns in 2008 and 2012 signaled a paradigm change in political campaigning. These campaigns made use of internet organizing tools, social media, and data analytics to organize grassroots activities, foster a feeling of community, and deliver messages that were specifically targeted to various voter categories. These campaigns' influence on the political scene continues to reverberate, influencing following ones and establishing new benchmarks for digital campaigning. The lessons discovered from Obama's digital campaigns serve as a testimony to the revolutionary potential of digital technologies in influencing the future of political involvement as technology continues to advance.

10.2 Trump's 2016 campaign and its digital strategies

Campaign tactics in the 2016 US presidential election saw a striking change, notably in how social media and digital technologies were used. Businessman and television personality Donald J. Trump reached and interacted with voters in unprecedented numbers by using a variety of cutting-edge digital methods. This article examines Trump's 2016 campaign and the digital tactics used, emphasizing their influence on the outcome of the election and the change of political campaigning that followed.

With social media platforms becoming potent weapons for politicians, the 2016 election represented a turning point in political campaigns. The Trump campaign saw the potential of social media sites like Facebook, Twitter, and Instagram to reach millions of Americans directly with their message. The campaign attempted to bypass conventional media outlets and establish a direct relationship with voters by using these platforms.

The Trump campaign used data-driven targeting strategies to locate and interact with prospective supporters. An important part in this was performed by the now-defunct political consulting company Cambridge Analytica. The company used psychographic profiling methods, integrating information from several sources, including social media platforms, to create comprehensive profiles of each voter. This made it possible for the campaign to target certain groups with its content and commercials, greatly increasing their effect.

Recognizing that social media advertising might reach huge audiences for very little money, Trump's campaign team made significant investments in it. Based on the demographics, hobbies, and internet activity of certain voting groups, they used microtargeting methods to send tailored messaging. With this strategy, the campaign was able to maximize its advertising budget and produce significant interaction.

The core of Donald Trump's campaign's digital strategy evolved into his personal Twitter account. He attracted millions of followers thanks to his straightforward and uncensored communication style and utilized the platform to announce policies, address detractors, and energize his following. Trump's tweets quickly rose to the top of the news cycle, generating a steady stream of media attention that boosted his message and cemented his reputation as an outsider candidate.

The Trump campaign understood the value of creating an internet fan base. For the purpose of promoting interaction and creating a feeling of community among supporters, they made use of social media platforms and campaign websites. Trump's staff organized online events, created specialized Facebook groups, and supported volunteer-driven projects. By giving fans the tools to become brand ambassadors, the campaign's message could be shared with their social networks.

The use of user-generated material was a key component of Trump's internet approach. The initiative urged participants to produce and distribute original material, including films, memes, and testimonies. The campaign expanded its reach and authenticity by amplifying these grassroots initiatives, successfully using the zeal and ingenuity of its supporters.

Trump's campaign used important people and alternative media channels in addition to conventional media outlets. They located conservative bloggers, podcasters, and social media influencers who had sizable fan bases within their target demographics and got in touch with them. With this strategy, the campaign was able to reach out to already-existing communities and use reliable sources to spread its message further.

Trump's staff made good use of online channels to manage and address issues during the campaign. Through the use of real-time communication platforms like Twitter, they were able to quickly refute unfavorable stories, manage the media narrative, and refocus public attention. The effect of controversies was lessened and the public image was shaped by this reactive digital approach.

The usage of digital methods in political campaigns was changed by Trump's presidential campaign in 2016. Trump's team effectively connected with millions of people using data-driven targeting, social media savvy, and online community building. Utilizing influencers, user-generated material, and Twitter as a direct communication route, the campaign was able to further amplify its message. The Trump campaign's use of digital tactics in the 2016 election not only affected the results but also established a standard for future political campaigns, permanently altering the field of political communication and campaigning.

10.3 Macron's 2017 digital campaign and the use of data-driven campaigning

The ascent of Emmanuel Macron, a political outsider who successfully negotiated the challenging world of data-driven campaigning, was a defining feature of the 2017 French presidential election. The Macron campaign used sophisticated data analytics and cutting-edge technology to deliberately target voters, rally supporters, and craft messages. This article examines Macron's online campaign in 2017 and emphasizes the crucial role data-driven marketing tactics played in his win.

The vibrant and creative way that Emmanuel Macron ran for president, especially online, stood out in the field of candidates. In order to make up for his lack of established party infrastructure as a centrist candidate, Macron understood the need of using technology and analytics. His campaign used social media, digital platforms, and data-driven strategies to directly approach voters, building a unique brand and enlisting a wide range of supporters.

Facebook, Twitter, and Instagram were all successfully used by Macron's campaign to interact with people, spread campaign messaging, and create a feeling of community. The marketing team produced interesting material that appealed to youthful and tech-savvy consumers, including films, graphics, and live streaming. Macron's team promoted a feeling of authenticity and accessibility by actively interacting with users, presenting Macron as a candidate who understood and welcomed the digital age.

The fact that Macron's internet campaign was data-driven was one of its main advantages. Massive volumes of voter data were collected and analyzed by Macron's team using cutting-edge data analytics methods. They were able to target certain voting groups, uncover important demographics, and create messaging that spoke to people's unique worries and goals by making use of this data. This individualized strategy improved the success of Macron's campaign by enabling him to relate to people on a more intimate and emotional level.

Using the information gleaned through data analysis, Macron's team used microtargeting techniques to send customized messages and adverts to certain voter groupings. Macron's team was able to maximize campaign spending by concentrating resources on voters who were most likely to be responsive to their message by analyzing the preferences, interests, and online habits of various voting groupings. With this strategy, the campaign was able to optimize its effect while lowering its expenditures, creating a highly effective and focused effort.

Additionally, data-driven advertising was very important in gaining popular support for Macron's candidacy. The campaign used data analytics to locate prospective volunteers and donors, then reached out to them personally to engage them. They promoted user-generated content, enabled networking, and organized neighborhood activities by using social media and internet platforms. An passionate and engaged campaign base was produced as a consequence of this grassroots mobilization, which gave supporters a feeling of empowerment and ownership.

Fighting misinformation and false news has become a serious problem for political candidates in the age of internet campaigning. The Macron campaign was aware of this issue and used data-driven tactics to detect and dispel misleading information. They were able to spot popular misinformation operations and react quickly with fact-checking, explanations, and alternative narratives by keeping an eye on social media platforms and using sentiment analysis. By being proactive, Macron was able to preserve the integrity of his campaign and increase voter confidence.

With its demonstration of the revolutionary potential of data-driven techniques, Macron's digital campaign in 2017 represents a paradigm leap in political campaigning. The success of the campaign illustrated how crucial it is to use technology, social media, and data analytics to successfully engage voters, target important demographics, and enlist grassroots support. In addition, Macron's strategy emphasized the need of privacy, transparency, and responsibility, underlining the necessity for ethical concerns in data-driven campaigning.

Through the use of data-driven tactics, Emmanuel Macron's 2017 digital campaign transformed political campaigning. Macron's team successfully interacted with voters, generated grassroots support, and fought misinformation through using social media, utilizing modern data analytics, and using tailored messaging. Future political campaigns will be affected significantly by the lessons learnt from Macron's campaign, which emphasize the importance of data-driven campaigning in determining election results and the need for ethical standards in the digital sphere. Data-driven campaigning will continue to be an essential tool for political candidates looking to engage with people in a world that is becoming more connected and digital as technology develops.

10.4 Analyzing the impact and lessons learned from these digital campaigns

Analysis of the effects and takeaways from the digital campaigns of Emmanuel Macron, Donald Trump, and Barack Obama might provide important insights into how political communication and campaigning are changing. To engage people, rally support, and sway public opinion, these three leaders made use of internet channels. In this research, we'll look at the unique traits and tactics that each campaign used, the effect they had on the elections in question, and the lessons that may be learned from both their triumphs and failures.

Political campaigning was transformed by Barack Obama's use of digital media during the 2008 and 2012 U.S. presidential elections. Early on, Obama saw the promise of social media and used sites like Facebook, Twitter, and YouTube to mobilize the general public. His team concentrated on developing a feeling of community and a dialog with supporters. To successfully engage certain voter segments, they used data-driven targeting and individualized messaging. Obama's "Yes We Can" slogan and "Hope" campaign poster were enduring representations of his message, and they went viral on social media, expanding his audience and motivating his supporters.

In order to generate record-breaking sums of money, Obama's digital campaign also used cutting-edge fundraising strategies including online contributions and micro-targeted email mailings. They created an advanced digital infrastructure that gave volunteers the ability to plan events, communicate with voters, and distribute campaign materials. Further enhancing his attractiveness and authenticity, Obama's campaign staff embraced storytelling and created appealing internet videos, including his well-known address on race in America.

During the 2016 U.S. presidential election, Donald Trump's digital campaign used a totally different strategy. Trump saw the potential of social media as an open and direct conduit for communication. His campaign staff mostly used Twitter to communicate with supporters and disseminate messages. Trump was able to dominate news cycles and shape the election narrative as a result of his aggressive and divisive tweets, which attracted considerable media attention. He interacted directly with his base instead than using the conventional media, which he often attacked, which helped to create a strong feeling of participation and devotion.

Targeted advertising and data analytics were other key components of Trump's campaign. They made extensive use of social media channels like Facebook to send personalized messaging to tiny voting groups. Through this strategy, they were able to connect with prospective supporters that more conventional campaigns would have missed. Trump's campaign also used innovative strategies that helped him reach specialized audiences, such as digital advertising on sites like Reddit.

The effectiveness of internet organization and grassroots mobilization was proved by Emmanuel Macron's digital campaign during the 2017 French presidential election. At the time, Macron was a relatively unknown political newcomer who used internet channels to create a large movement and engage dissatisfied people. His campaign staff made heavy use of social media, using both organic content and targeted advertising to reach a variety of voter categories. They highlighted Macron's plans for a contemporary and inclusive France, especially appealing to younger people.

The emphasis of Macron's campaign was on developing a strong internet presence and encouraging participation. They enlisted the help of supporters to turn them into "digital volunteers" who could disseminate campaign information, plan events, and interact with prospective voters. Additionally, Macron's team used data analytics to learn more about voter preferences and behavior, which allowed them to improve their outreach and message strategies. Additionally, by using live-streamed occasions like town hall meetings and debates, Macron was able to interact with his followers directly and respond to their issues in real-time.

A review of these digital marketing' results teaches us some vital truths. First and foremost, strong awareness of the target demographic and the channels they use is necessary for successful digital advertising. Obama, Trump, and Macron all understood the need of customizing their messaging and approaches to appeal to certain voter categories. Second, in order to engage voters, honesty and narrative are essential. Trump's blunt communication style, Obama's message of optimism, and Macron's call for change all found favor with their different support groups. Thirdly, digital marketing initiatives must be flexible and adaptable. Campaigns must adopt new technology, experiment with novel strategies, and remain ahead of the curve due to the continually shifting nature of digital platforms.

These commercials also emphasize the significance of targeting and data analytics. Effective data exploitation allows campaigns to pinpoint critical swing voters, micro-target message, and maximize resource use. But it's also important to consider the moral consequences of data consumption and privacy issues. Furthermore, competent digital campaigning techniques are required due to the effects of social media echo chambers and the possibility for disinformation to proliferate quickly.

In conclusion, Barack Obama, Donald Trump, and Emmanuel Macron's digital campaigns had a significant influence on their respective elections and changed the political communication environment. Their methods and tactics showed the effectiveness of data analytics, social media, and grassroots mobilization. Each campaign provides useful lessons for upcoming political candidates and campaigners, from Obama's community-driven strategy to Trump's disruptive use of Twitter and Macron's emphasis on diversity. Political actors may more effectively traverse the complicated digital terrain to communicate with voters, affect public opinion, and eventually win elections by recognizing the advantages and disadvantages of these digital campaigns.

Chapter 11

The Future of Digital Political Campaigns: Opportunities and Challenges

11. Introduction

Political candidates and parties now face both possibilities and problems as a result of the revolutionary changes brought about by digital technology. The growth of digital political campaigns is anticipated to continue in the future, changing the nature of election processes all over the globe. We will look at the possible advantages and difficulties that digital political campaigns may face in this article.

Opportunities:

- Broader Reach and Engagement: Political campaigns have an unrivaled potential to reach and interact with a bigger audience thanks to digital media. In particular, social media gives candidates a direct access to people, promoting in-person encounters and solidifying online networks. Furthermore, campaigns may adapt their messaging to certain demographics to increase their reach and effect by using data analytics and targeted advertising.

- Enhanced Voter Mobilization: Digital technologies provide campaigns the ability to more effectively organize voters. By identifying prospective supporters with the use of sophisticated data analytics and machine learning algorithms, campaigns may customize messaging and create micro-targeted tactics. Additionally, social networking sites and smartphone apps provide direct voter outreach, aiding in attempts to find volunteers and register voters.

- Enhanced Transparency: Digital campaigns have the potential to improve political process transparency. Candidates may participate in open discussions, submit comprehensive policy ideas, and reveal their campaign financing using internet forums. Additionally, cutting-edge technology like blockchain show promise in assuring the legitimacy of political contributions and expenditures while minimizing the impact of dark money.

Challenges:

- Misinformation and False News: As a result of the expansion of digital platforms, there has also been an uptick in misinformation and fake news, which is a major problem for political campaigns. The ease of sharing information online may be used by malicious actors to promote misleading information and sway public opinion. In order to combat misinformation, campaigns must establish effective measures, such as fact-checking programs, media literacy efforts, and collaboration with digital firms to enforce content moderation regulations.

- Data security and privacy: Data security and privacy issues are brought up by political campaigns' extensive collecting and use of personal information. The improper manipulation or exploitation of data may undermine public confidence and have negative effects on campaigns. Regulations on data protection and transparency must be put into place and followed by campaigns in order to solve this issue. Additionally, to protect campaign infrastructure and stop data breaches, investing in strong cybersecurity measures is crucial.

- Technological Inequality: Although digital campaigns provide a wealth of potential, the digital gap still poses a serious obstacle. Not everyone has access to the internet equally or has the essential digital literacy abilities. This inequality may result in uneven political engagement, keeping certain groups of people from participating in politics. Political campaigns must deal with this problem by supporting programs for digital inclusion and providing other ways for individuals with restricted internet access to participate.

Future digital political campaigns have the power to drastically alter the electoral environment. The chances for a broader audience, better voting turnout, and more transparency are alluring. To guarantee the integrity and inclusion of digital political campaigns, it is necessary to adequately address the issues of misinformation, data privacy, and technical disparity. Political players, legislators, and society as a whole must actively participate in determining the future of digital political campaigns as technology develops, working toward a democratic and equitable digital political environment.

11.1 Exploring emerging technologies and their potential impact on digital campaigns

The realm of marketing and advertising is just one area of our life that has been significantly impacted by the quickly changing technological environment. Digital campaigns have seen a substantial transition in recent years as a result of the introduction of innovative technology. This article looks at a number of cutting-edge technologies and how they could affect online advertising. We can learn more about the prospects for marketing and advertising in the future by looking at the advantages and difficulties brought on by these technologies.

A game-changer in the world of digital marketing is artificial intelligence. Marketing professionals are now able to examine massive volumes of data and get insightful knowledge about customer behavior thanks to AI-powered technology like machine learning algorithms and natural language processing. As a result, marketing initiatives may be more specialized and focused, which improves client retention and conversion rates. Chatbots and virtual assistants may now provide individualized consumer experiences, offering real-time support and raising customer happiness thanks to AI.

The use of AI in digital marketing, however, is not without its difficulties. AI algorithms that gather and use personal data raise privacy issues and ethical questions. To ensure that customer data is handled sensibly and openly, marketers must find a balance between customization and privacy. Additionally, to remain on top of the curve, marketers must constantly upgrade their knowledge and abilities due to the fast evolution of AI technology.

By giving customers immersive and engaging experiences, virtual reality and augmented reality technologies have the potential to change digital advertising. While AR projects digital material over the actual world, VR immerses viewers in a virtual realm. These technologies may be used by marketers to exhibit their goods, provide virtual tours, and engage people in interesting ways.

For instance, a furniture company may utilize augmented reality to let clients see a piece of furniture in their homes before making a purchase. This improves shopping and lessens the possibility of returns. Similar to how it may be used to imitate experiences that are difficult to duplicate practically, like test driving a vehicle or seeing a new place, VR can be used to build virtual showrooms.

However, issues like cost and accessibility limit the use of VR and AR in digital advertisements. Larger firms can only embrace VR and AR since it demands a lot of resources to provide high-quality experiences. Furthermore, the need for specialist technology, such as VR headsets, may prevent mainstream consumer adoption. These difficulties should disappear as technology improves and becomes more accessible.

The network of networked objects with sensors and software that enable them to gather and share data is referred to as the "Internet of Things." IoT campaign integration gives marketers new ways to collect real-time data and provide customized experiences. For instance, data on customer behavior and preferences may be provided through smart home devices, allowing marketers to adjust their campaigns as necessary.

IoT also makes it possible for marketers to target customers based on their actual proximity to a particular area. This may be used for interactive experiences, tailored suggestions, and targeted advertising. However, IoT device privacy and security issues are a major factor to take into account. To gain the confidence of their target audience, marketers must make sure that customer data is protected and that their data methods are open and honest.

The way people seek for information and engage with technology has changed as voice-enabled gadgets and smart assistants like Amazon Alexa and Google Assistant gain popularity. Digital campaigns must now optimize their content for speech-based inquiries as a result of the move toward voice search. Adapting keywords, comprehending natural language use patterns, and responding to user questions with clear, correct responses are all part of voice search optimization.

Additionally, smart assistants provide new chances for marketers to interact with customers. For smart assistants, brands may create voice-activated skills or applications that offer tailored information and services. However, there are issues with competitiveness and discoverability in voice search results. Marketers must modify their SEO tactics to account for voice-based inquiries and research cutting-edge approaches to get users' attention in a voice-driven environment.

Digital campaigns are changing as a result of emerging technology, which are giving marketers new tools and chances to interact with customers. One example of a technology that has the potential to change marketing and advertising is artificial intelligence. Other examples include virtual reality, augmented reality, the internet of things, voice search, and smart assistants. Even though these technologies have many advantages, issues with privacy, cost, accessibility, and competitiveness need to be resolved. Marketers are likely to acquire a competitive advantage in the fast-paced world of digital marketing if they adopt these new technologies and modify their plans appropriately.

11.2 Predictive modeling and its role in shaping digital campaign strategies

By using historical data and statistical methods to forecast the future, predictive modeling plays a significant role in designing digital advertising tactics. Businesses are using the potential of predictive modeling to enhance their digital marketing efforts and produce better outcomes as a consequence of the fast evolution of technology and the growing availability of data. We will go into the idea of predictive modeling and consider its importance in building digital marketing tactics in this article.

Statistical models for prediction of future events or behaviors based on patterns in past data are created via the process of predictive modeling. These models are created utilizing sophisticated algorithms and machine learning approaches, allowing organizations to predict consumer behavior and make data-driven choices. Predictive models may find significant connections and trends that may not be obvious to people by evaluating enormous volumes of data, including consumer demographics, browsing habits, purchase histories, and social media interactions.

Predictive modeling provides useful insights into several elements of marketing, including consumer segmentation, targeting, personalisation, and campaign optimization, in the context of digital campaign tactics. Businesses may adjust their campaigns to give more relevant and interesting information by studying the traits and preferences of various client categories. Predictive models can pinpoint the major variables that affect consumer behavior, enabling marketers to develop specialized offers and messages that appeal to certain market groups.

Customer segmentation is one of the main uses of predictive modeling in digital marketing strategy. Businesses may better understand their audience and focus their marketing efforts by classifying clients into separate groups based on their characteristics and actions. Customers may be divided into groups based on variables like age, gender, geography, purchase history, and browsing habits using predictive models that analyze consumer data to uncover common traits. With the help of this segmentation, marketers can develop highly focused ads that appeal to certain client categories, increasing engagement and conversion rates.

Predictive modeling is also essential for consumer targeting. Businesses may determine which customers are most likely to be interested in their goods or services by combining historical data with prediction algorithms. To determine the chance of conversion or engagement, predictive algorithms may evaluate several consumer qualities and behaviors and offer a probability score to each prospect. Then, marketers may concentrate their efforts on focusing their efforts on contacting the prospects with the greatest likelihood ratings, perfecting their digital marketing methods, and maximizing their return on investment.

Predictive modeling has a big influence on digital marketing tactics in the field of personalization as well. Customers increasingly want tailored services and information that is relevant to their individual requirements and tastes. Predictive models may examine the specific information about a client, such as previous purchases, browsing patterns, and demographic data, to forecast their future preferences and provide tailored offers or content. Businesses may greatly improve customer engagement and increase conversion rates by personalizing the marketing message for each consumer.

Predictive modeling is essential to refining digital marketing tactics in addition to client segmentation, targeting, and personalisation. Predictive models may examine previous campaign data to pinpoint the crucial elements that either make a campaign successful or unsuccessful. Marketers may improve the performance of their next campaigns by studying the effects of several factors including timing, message, channel choice, and creative components. To reach their marketing objectives, marketers may make data-driven choices, efficiently manage their resources, and modify campaign settings with the use of predictive modeling.

Customer churn prediction and retention is an important area where predictive modeling is being used to shape digital advertising strategy. Predictive models may find trends and signs that point to probable churn by examining prior client data. Then, by providing tailored incentives, focused promotions, or proactive customer service, marketers may take proactive steps to keep clients. With the use of predictive modeling, organizations can identify at-risk clients and develop customized retention plans, lowering churn rates and boosting general client loyalty.

Predictive modeling may also help with budget allocation and digital advertising strategy improvement. Predictive models can forecast the effects of potential budget allocations across multiple marketing channels by examining past campaign data and performance indicators. This makes it possible for marketers to allocate their budgets most profitably and accomplish their campaign goals. Businesses can make sure that their digital advertising plans are affordable and get the required outcomes by determining the most successful channels and allocating money appropriately.

Predictive modeling, which uses historical data and statistical methods to create precise forecasts about the future, is essential for designing digital advertising tactics. Businesses may efficiently segment their client bases, target the most promising leads, customize their marketing campaigns, enhance their performance, forecast customer churn, and manage their resources by applying predictive models. Predictive modeling will become more important in helping firms remain ahead in the cutthroat digital environment and fuel effective marketing efforts as technology develops and more data becomes accessible.

11.3 The role of virtual reality and augmented reality in digital political campaigns

Political campaigns are no exception to the way that digital technology has altered numerous facets of our life. In the world of digital political campaigns, virtual reality (VR) and augmented reality (AR) have become potent weapons that provide voters and politicians immersive and interesting experiences. This article examines the possible effects, advantages, difficulties, and moral issues around the use of VR and AR in political campaigns.

Through the use of specialized headgear and controllers, people may interact with a virtual reality world. On the other hand, augmented reality, which is often accessible via smartphones or smart glasses, superimposes digital material over the actual environment. Both technologies provide distinctive means of reaching voters and spreading political views.

Voters may participate more fully with political campaigns thanks to the immersive and interactive experiences that VR and AR technology provide. Voters may digitally join rallies, discussions, or town hall meetings with VR, extending participation and overcoming physical constraints. On the other side, AR enables politicians to deploy digital signs and campaign materials in actual places, effectively and individually engaging with prospective voters.

Candidates may host virtual rallies and events to attract a larger audience by integrating VR and AR into their campaigns. Voters may virtually join the audience, take in talks, and engage with other participants via VR, imitating an actual experience. With AR, politicians may overlay campaign materials like posters and banners in numerous real-world areas, giving their campaigns a widespread presence.

Voters may be informed about complicated policy topics in an engaging and immersive fashion using VR and AR. Voters may feel the effects of various policy initiatives and see their results via VR simulations. Voters may quickly obtain pertinent information and encourage educated decision-making by using augmented reality to overlay educational images and data onto real-world items.

Politicians may now provide individualized campaign messages that connect with specific people by using VR and AR. Candidates may customize their VR and AR experiences to correspond with particular interests and concerns by studying voter data and preferences. This tailored strategy improves voter participation and forges closer ties between candidates and their supporters.

The ways that political campaigns generate money and solicit contributions may change as a result of VR and AR. Politicians may bring contributors to virtual fundraising events with realistic VR experiences, evoking a feeling of presence and urgency. Incorporating digital connections and reminders onto real-world things using augmented reality may help streamline the donation process and make it more convenient for prospective contributors.

While VR and AR have many advantages for political campaigns, ethical issues must be taken into account. Personal data collection and use for customized experiences raise privacy issues. Another significant concern that calls for strict regulation and control is the misuse of VR and AR technology to propagate false information or influence elections. To guarantee the proper use of new technologies in political campaigns, transparency and accountability procedures must be put in place.

The accessibility of the required gear is one issue with using VR and AR in political campaigns. As these technologies advance, efforts should be taken to guarantee that everyone has access to VR headsets and AR-capable gadgets. To avoid a digital gap in political activity, it will be essential to promote affordability and inclusion.

Voters are ultimately intended to be empowered and assisted in making educated decisions via the use of VR and AR in political campaigns. By bridging the gap between elected officials and their citizens, these technologies might promote a more interesting and dynamic political dialogue. VR and AR may support a more democratic and participatory society by promoting understanding and debate.

With the potential to increase voter participation, personalize campaign message, and encourage informed decision-making, virtual reality and augmented reality provide intriguing opportunities for political campaigns. However, it is still crucial to address ethical issues, technical accessibility, and responsible use. The immersive experiences of VR and AR might have a transformational effect on the political landscape of the future as technology advances.

11.4 Ethical considerations and policy implications for the future digital political campaigns

Political campaigns are increasingly using digital platforms and technology as effective methods for reaching and interacting with voters in the digital age. The political environment has undergone tremendous change as a result of the quick development of technology, but there are also moral questions and practical ramifications that need to be resolved. The goal of this article is to investigate the moral issues and political ramifications of upcoming digital political campaigns.

Data privacy and protection are one of the main ethical issues in online political campaigns. Numerous pieces of information on an individual's personal life, political beliefs, and internet activities are collected throughout campaigns. To avoid unauthorized access or abuse, policies must be set to control the collection, storage, and use of this data. In order to ensure that people understand how their data will be used and have the option to opt-out if wanted, transparency and informed consent should be prioritized.

Political campaigns may use customized advertising and microtargeting strategies on digital platforms to target certain voting categories. While this may increase the effectiveness of a campaign, it raises moral concerns about the possibility for discriminatory acts and the manipulation of public opinion. To guarantee openness in ad targeting algorithms and to stop the spread of inaccurate or misleading information to voters, more rules should be put in place. Additionally, efforts should be taken to prevent discriminatory targeting methods from maintaining social, economic, or racial inequities.

Concerns about algorithmic bias and manipulation develop when algorithmic technologies are used in digital campaigns more and more. Information bubbles and polarization may result from algorithms unintentionally amplifying extreme perspectives or reinforcing preexisting prejudices. To create algorithms that are open, impartial, and fair, policymakers should collaborate with tech firms. To identify and correct any instances of algorithmic manipulation or abuse, auditing and monitoring measures should be put in place.

A critical concern in online political campaigns is the spread of misinformation and false news. Viral social media platforms may be used by malicious actors to disseminate false information, sway public opinion, and compromise the integrity of democratic processes. To detect and counteract misinformation, policymakers must work with technology businesses to create successful tactics. Steps to solve this issue include improved openness in internet political advertising, media literacy programs, and fact-checking projects.

Online abuse and harassment are not unheard of in digital political campaigns. Threats, libel, and personal assaults on political candidates and their followers may prevent open and honest political debate. Policies should be implemented to safeguard people against harassment and set out penalties for offenders. Online platforms should also improve their moderation tools so they can spot and stop abuse faster.

Political campaigns conducted online must take into account the digital divide and accessibility difficulties that may prevent certain groups of people from fully engaging in the political process. By enhancing internet accessibility and digital literacy in marginalized areas, policies should place a priority on closing the digital divide. Political campaigns should also make sure that their digital material complies with accessibility standards and guidelines and is usable by people with impairments.

Discussions on ethical issues and their legislative repercussions must be at the forefront as digital political campaigns develop. Key issues that need addressing include data privacy and security, targeted advertising, algorithmic bias, misinformation, online abuse, and accessibility. We can create a digital campaign environment that upholds democratic values, ensures fairness, and safeguards the integrity of the political process for future generations by establishing clear regulations, promoting transparency, and encouraging collaboration between policymakers and technology companies.

Chapter 12

Conclusion

12. Introduction

The article "Pixels and Politicians," which examines the influence of computer science on political campaigns, has shed light on the revolutionary role that technology plays in contemporary politics. This study's research shows how computer science has substantially impacted political campaigns, changing how politicians interact with people, communicate with them, collect data, and form public opinion. It is clear from a thorough analysis of many different factors, such as social media, data analytics, and online advertising, that computer science has developed into a crucial tool for political campaigns, allowing politicians to reach a wider audience, customize their messages, and improve their strategies.

As social media sites like Facebook, Twitter, and Instagram have grown in popularity, politicians now have direct contact with millions of prospective voters. They can have dialogues in real time, promote their thoughts and initiatives, and get support like never before thanks to social media. The data shows that effective politicians make use of social media to engage with voters on a more personal level, cultivating a feeling of authenticity and approachability. The ability to analyze social media data, pinpoint influential individuals, and customize messaging for certain demographic groups has been made possible by computer science, which has improved the efficiency of political campaigns.

The report also emphasizes the substantial influence of data analytics on political campaigns. Large-scale data collecting, processing, and interpretation have been made easier thanks to computer science, enabling campaigns to create focused plans and make informed choices. Politicians may learn a lot about voter behavior, preferences, and emotion by using machine learning algorithms and predictive modeling. They may use this to create campaign communications that appeal to certain voter groups, maximize resource use, and even reasonably anticipate election results. Political campaigns have become more sophisticated as a result of the integration of computer science and data analytics, evolving from intuitive undertakings into strategic endeavors informed by empirical facts.

The research also examines the function of internet advertising in political campaigns, which is another important topic. Politicians may accurately target their adverts to certain demographics and geographic areas thanks to the rise of digital platforms and ad technology, increasing the effect of their campaign expenditures. The development of advanced ad targeting algorithms made possible by computer science allows for the delivery of targeted messages to prospective voters by using user data, browser history, and online activity. Politicians may foster a feeling of connection and relevance by customizing their adverts based on individual tastes, raising the possibility of voter participation and support. Younger groups, who are more likely to be engaged online and open to digital campaigns, have found to be especially influenced by this factor.

The rising use of computer science in political campaigns raises both prospective difficulties and ethical issues that must be acknowledged. Consideration must be given carefully to critical problems such privacy concerns, data security, and the possibility for manipulation. As computer science develops, it is essential for legislators and campaign strategists to set up strict norms and moral standards to guarantee accountability, transparency, and fairness in the use of technology during campaigns.

The book "Pixels and Politicians" examines how computer science has affected political campaigns, highlighting the enormous effect that technology has had on contemporary politics. The way politicians engage with people, acquire data, and sway public opinion has been changed by the incorporation of computer science tools and methods including social media, data analytics, and online advertising. The results show how computer science may help with focused outreach, data-driven decision-making, and customised communication. The ethical ramifications and possible dangers of using technology in political campaigns must be addressed, however. Policymakers and campaign strategists may embrace the potential of computer technology while respecting democratic norms and guaranteeing a fair and transparent political process by accepting ethical practices and laws.

The research "Pixels and Politicians" emphasizes the significance of computer science in grassroots organization and mobilization efforts inside political campaigns in addition to the results listed above. Campaign activities have become more effective and broad because to the creative ways that technology has made it possible for volunteers and supporters to organize and work together. Volunteers may now plan events, exchange information, and find new supporters thanks to digital platforms and communication technologies, which has eventually increased the effect and reach of political campaigns. The development of user-friendly online and mobile systems that simplify voter registration, volunteer management, and get-out-the-vote campaigns has been made possible by computer science. By fusing grassroots organization with technology, historically disadvantaged groups have become more engaged and involved, promoting a more inclusive democratic process.

The research also explores the issue of algorithmic bias and its possible effects on political campaigns. There is a chance that current prejudices and inequities will continue to persist as computer science algorithms grow more and more crucial to campaign decision-making processes. The predictions and suggestions that algorithms make are based on previous data, which might unintentionally perpetuate biased behaviors or omit certain groups from focused outreach. Campaign strategists and technology developers must take steps to address and counteract algorithmic biases so that justice, equality, and representation are upheld in the design and use of computer science tools.

In addition, the paper acknowledges the importance of computer technology in battling false information during political campaigns. The integrity of democratic processes is seriously threatened by the quick spread of misleading information and the swaying of public opinion. Computer technology, however, provides creative ways to counter disinformation, such as natural language processing algorithms that can recognize and identify bogus news stories or social media bots. Campaigns may proactively attack false narratives and promote true information by using automated fact-checking technologies and data analytics to uncover trends of disinformation spread. Political campaigns may promote better democratic dialogue and an educated electorate by using computer science tools.

In order to further investigate the influence of computer science on political campaigns, the study highlights the necessity for continued research and cooperation between computer scientists, political scientists, policymakers, and other stakeholders. It is crucial to evaluate the effects of technology as it develops on democracy, individual rights, and the general efficiency of election procedures. Future political campaigns will be shaped by our ability to assess the advantages and disadvantages of new technologies like blockchain, virtual reality, and artificial intelligence.

In summary, "Pixels and Politicians" offers a thorough examination of the influence of computer science on political campaigns. It emphasizes how technology is transforming how campaigns are run, increasing voter participation, and allowing data-driven decision-making.

Political campaigns may benefit greatly from computer science, but ethical issues, algorithmic biases, and the problem of disinformation must all be taken into account. The fusion of computer science and politics may help to create an election process that is more inclusive, transparent, and democratic by adopting these principles. In order to navigate the always changing terrain of technology's influence on politics and ensure its beneficial effects on society, ongoing study and cooperation will be essential.

12.1 Summarizing the key findings and insights

Computer science has changed many industries in the era of quickly evolving technology, and politics is no exception. Politicians are now able to reach a broader audience, collect data-driven insights, and improve their campaigning techniques thanks to the merger of computer science and politics. This article examines the most important conclusions and revelations about how computer science affects political campaigns, emphasizing the revolutionary changes it makes to message, voter targeting, funding, and overall campaign efficiency.

The creation, dissemination, and reception of political messages have all been revolutionized by computer technology. Political candidates now have direct access to millions of prospective voters because to the development of social media and digital platforms. They may modify their messaging to appeal to certain populations, resulting in more individualized and focused communication.

Politicians are able to create communications that appeal to their target audience by using data analytics and technologies for natural language processing. Additionally, computer technology offers real-time public opinion monitoring, supporting quick reaction methods and enabling politicians to dynamically modify their messaging.

Computer technology is essential for locating and influencing prospective voters. Voter profiling has been transformed by cutting-edge data analytics and machine learning algorithms, allowing campaigns to more correctly analyze voters' preferences, behaviors, and demographics. Campaigns may adjust their agendas by identifying the major topics that matter to certain voter groups by analyzing enormous volumes of data. Additionally, computer technology makes microtargeting possible, enabling campaigns to send tailored messages to specific voters via digital channels and enhancing the effectiveness of their outreach efforts.

The world of political fundraising has undergone a dramatic transformation because to computer technology. Politicians now have additional channels for interacting with prospective contributors and rallying support thanks to online platforms and crowdfunding efforts. Advanced algorithms and predictive models aid in the identification of prospective contributors and the selection of the most efficient fundraising tactics. Large donor datasets may be analyzed by machine learning algorithms to forecast gift trends and improve fundraising tactics. Furthermore, computer science has made it easier to employ cryptocurrencies and blockchain technology for political fundraising, enabling procedures with speed, security, and transparency.

The total efficiency of political campaigns has been significantly increased thanks to computer technology. Campaigns may assess the effectiveness of their plans in real-time by using data analytics, enabling quick modifications and improvement. Campaigns may experiment with various messaging, platforms, and targeting strategies thanks to A/B testing and predictive modeling, which helps them find the best strategies for influencing and mobilizing voters. Additionally, computer science has transformed campaign management by simplifying procedures, automating repetitive work, and enhancing team collaboration, leading to more effective and data-driven decision-making processes.

The use of computer science in political campaigns has enormous advantages, but it also presents significant ethical questions. Huge volumes of personal data are being collected and used, which raises questions regarding data security and privacy. It is difficult to strike a balance between using data for successful campaigning and preserving individual privacy; this problem calls for strict rules and moral principles. Additionally, the danger of algorithmic bias and the capability of tailored messaging to sway public opinion underline the need of openness, responsibility, and ethical technology usage in political campaigns.

Political campaigns now use computer science to effectively target voters, engage with constituents, generate money, and operate efficient operations. Data analytics, machine learning, and digital platforms have made it possible to target voters precisely, provide tailored messages, raise money quickly, and make informed decisions. To guarantee openness, privacy, and justice, it is essential to address the ethical issues surrounding the use of technology in politics. To encourage democratic participation, informed decision-making, and a responsible use of technology in politics, further study and ongoing assessment of the influence of computer science on political campaigns are vital as technology develops.

The area of social media and online interaction is where computer technology has had one of the most profound effects on political campaigns. Politicians now rely heavily on websites like Facebook, Twitter, Instagram, and YouTube to communicate with people, disseminate their views, and rally support. Politicians may now reach large audiences with little effort because to computer science's role in the platforms' fast development and impact.

Artificial intelligence-powered social media algorithms are crucial in determining the kind of material that consumers see in their feeds. This offers political campaigns both chances and difficulties. On the one hand, depending on their interests, demographics, and online activity, these algorithms may assist campaigns in identifying and reaching out to certain voter groups. Campaigns may boost their exposure and foster a feeling of authenticity and relatability by proactively creating and marketing content.

The algorithms do, however, also present problems with polarization and the spread of information. Users may be exposed to material largely that supports their preexisting opinions and tastes, leading to the formation of echo chambers and filter bubbles. This may exacerbate political division and prevent the free interchange of ideas. Furthermore, the viral nature of social media may hasten the dissemination of incorrect information, necessitating strong debunking operations to guarantee accurate information reaches voters.

Through interactive elements like live streaming, chatbots, and online forums, computer technology has also changed how people connect online. Town halls and events may be live streamed, which enables politicians to interact with voters directly, respond to inquiries in real time, and encourage participation. Chatbots provide pre-written solutions to frequently asked questions, facilitating conversation and guaranteeing prompt involvement. Voters may communicate with one another, exchange ideas, and engage in political conversation on online discussion boards and forums, which promotes a feeling of community and political engagement.

Advanced social media analytics have also been made possible by computer science, enabling campaigns to track engagement metrics, sentiment analysis, and audience demographics. Campaigns may use these information to gauge the success of their social media tactics, spot patterns, and improve their message plans. Campaigns can adapt their content, find prominent voices, and use social media to rally support and increase voter participation by knowing the internet environment.

Thoughts about false information, privacy, and the possibility of manipulation are also raised by the growth of social media and online participation in political campaigns. The legitimacy of the democratic process is put in jeopardy by the proliferation of false information and the promotion of extreme viewpoints. By fostering media literacy, fact-checking, and appropriate use of social media platforms, political campaigns need to address these issues. Additionally, guaranteeing user data privacy and ensuring transparency in political advertising are essential measures in preserving public confidence and creating a fair and informed voting environment.

Through the use of social media and internet participation, computer technology has changed political campaigns. These platforms have allowed for tailored message, direct interaction, and real-time data, giving politicians access to voters that has never before been possible. However, to maintain the honesty and fairness of political campaigns, the ethical issues raised by social media algorithms, false information, and privacy violations must be properly managed. Politicians may use social media and online interaction to promote democratic participation, bridge gaps, and build a more educated and involved electorate by using the promise of computer technology while preserving ethical norms.

12.3 Examining the implications for the future of democracy

Modern political landscapes now inextricably include digital campaigning, revolutionizing how politicians interact with people and sway public opinion. The use of tailored messaging, data analytics, and social media platforms has completely changed how political campaigns are run. While there are many potential for politicians to engage with voters and garner support via digital campaigning, there are also various ramifications for the future of democracy. This article explores both the advantages and disadvantages of internet campaigning as well as any possible repercussions on the political process.

The ability of digital campaigning to improve inclusion and accessibility in the political process is one of its main benefits. Politicians may communicate with a larger audience, interact directly with voters, and disseminate information about their political agendas and policies thanks to social media platforms and digital technologies. By making conventional political procedures more accessible, minority groups and those who may have previously been shut out of them may become more powerful. Digital platforms may also encourage public involvement and enhance political dialogue, promoting active participation in democratic discourse.

Misinformation and disinformation provide a difficulty for digital campaigns as well. False stories and rumors may spread swiftly thanks to social media's speedy dissemination of information, impacting public opinion and weakening the democratic process. Election integrity and the public's capacity for making informed judgments are seriously threatened by the ease with which false information may be produced and spread. By exposing people exclusively to material that supports their preexisting opinions, filter bubbles and echo chambers, which are common, further aggravate this problem and cause polarization and a lack of critical thinking.

Huge volumes of personal data are gathered and used during digital campaigns, which raises privacy issues and the possibility of manipulation. Complex data analytics are often used in political campaigns to target certain groups and modify messaging appropriately. While this may increase the effectiveness of campaigns, it also raises moral concerns about privacy invasion and the possibility for manipulation via micro-targeting strategies. Utilizing personal information might result in highly customized and sometimes deceptive political ads, further undermining faith in the democratic process.

The financial effects of digital campaigning are enormous, and they change the political power dynamics. The proliferation of online political expenditures may not be fully addressed by conventional campaign funding restrictions, potentially resulting in unequal distribution of campaign resources. Digital spaces may possibly be dominated by wealthy candidates or interest groups with access to significant finance, drowning out the views of candidates with less means. This disparity threatens the democratic ideal of equal representation and lessens the voice of common people in politics.

The distribution of divisive information and the reach of extreme ideology have been aided by the internet environment. Social media algorithms often favor interesting and information that is debatable, unintentionally fostering extreme views. Increasing polarization might result from algorithmic amplification because people are exposed to material that confirms their own opinions and distances them from competing viewpoints. The ensuing echo chambers and the increase in online hate speech provide serious obstacles to promoting free and open discussion, undermining the values of democratic compromise and debate.

Regulations have not kept up with the quick development of digital campaigning, which has created a gap in accountability. The difficulty for governments and politicians is to create effective legislation to deal with the moral, legal, and transparent challenges related to digital campaign techniques. It is necessary to take proactive steps to address issues like online political advertising transparency, data privacy, and the duty of social media platforms to stop the spread of disinformation in order to strike a balance between the need for campaign innovation and safeguarding the democratic process. Securing the future of democracy in the digital era requires finding the ideal balance between regulation and the protection of free expression.

Digital campaigning has completely changed the way politics is conducted by opening up new channels for political participation and mobilization. Its effects for the future of democracy, however, are intricate and diverse.

While digital campaigning improves accessibility and diversity, it also has drawbacks, including polarization, financial inequality, disinformation, and privacy problems. In order to address these issues, a comprehensive strategy that incorporates legal frameworks, technology advancement, media literacy campaigns, and ethical behavior on social media platforms is necessary. We must overcome these obstacles to keep the democratic process open, inclusive, and robust if we want democracy to survive in the digital era.

References:

1. Bennett, W. L., & Segerberg, A. (2012). The logic of connective action: Digital media and the personalization of contentious politics. Information, Communication & Society, 15(5), 739-768.

2. Bimber, B. (2019). Digital media in the Obama campaigns of 2008 and 2012: Adaptation to the personalized political communication environment. Political Communication, 36(3), 460-481.

3. Chadwick, A. (2017). The hybrid media system: Politics and power. Oxford University Press.

4. Davis, R., & Owen, D. (2018). Cybersecurity and the 2016 US Presidential Elections. Journal of Policy and Complex Systems, 2(2), 145-165.

5. Enli, G. S., & Skogerbø, E. (2013). Personalized campaigns in party-centred politics: Twitter and Facebook as arenas for political communication. Information, Communication & Society, 16(5), 757-774.

6. Faris, R., Roberts, H., & Etling, B. (2017). Partisanship, propaganda, and disinformation:

Online media and the 2016 US Presidential Election. Berkman Klein Center for Internet & Society Research Paper, (2017-6).

7. Karpf, D. (2012). The MoveOn effect: The unexpected transformation of American political advocacy. Oxford University Press.

8. Kreiss, D. (2016). Prototype politics: Technology-intensive campaigning and the data of democracy. Oxford University Press.

9. Lilleker, D. G., Koc-Michalska, K., & Schweitzer, E. J. (2019). Presidential Campaigning and Social Media: An Analysis of the 2018 German Party Communication on Facebook and Twitter. Social Media + Society, 5(2), 2056305119841436.

10. Trielli, D., & Gaffney, D. (2019). Digital advertising in political campaigns: The impact of Facebook political ads on candidate evaluation. Information, Communication & Society, 22(5), 700-716.

11. Margolis, M., & Resnick, D. (Eds.). (2018). Politics as usual: The cyberspace revolution. Sage Publications.

12. Metz, C. (2018). AI-powered politics and the manipulation of information. Nature Machine Intelligence, 1(9), 429-431.

13. Nisbet, M. C., & Scheufele, D. A. (2004). Political talk as a catalyst for online citizenship. Journalism

& Mass Communication Quarterly, 81(4), 877-896.

14. Parmelee, J. H., & Bichard, S. L. (2011). Politics and the Twitter revolution: How tweets influence the relationship between political leaders and the public. Lanham, MD: Lexington Books.

15. Raynauld, V., & Greenberg, J. (2017). Digital politics in Canada: Towards a comparative framework. Canadian Journal of Political Science, 50(2), 489-514.

16. Tumasjan, A., Sprenger, T. O., Sandner, P. G., & Welpe, I. M. (2010). Predicting elections with Twitter: What 140 characters reveal about political sentiment. ICWSM, 10(1), 178-185.

17. Vaccari, C., Valeriani, A., Barberá, P., Bonneau, R., Jost, J. T., Nagler, J., ... & Tucker, J. A. (2020). How populists wage social media campaigns. Information, Communication & Society, 23(5), 703-729.

18. Vargo, C. J., & Guo, L. (2017). Networks, big data, and intermedia agenda-setting: An analysis of traditional, partisan, and emerging online US news. Journalism & Mass Communication Quarterly, 94(4), 1037-1058.

19. Walter, A. S., & Passarelli, A. (2019). Computational propaganda: A political economy perspective. Digital Journalism, 7(6), 772-791.

20. Woolley, S. C., & Howard, P. N. (Eds.). (2018). Computational propaganda: Political parties, politicians, and political manipulation on social media. Oxford University Press.

21. Kreiss, D. (2014). Seizing the moment: The presidential campaigns' use of Twitter during the 2012 electoral cycle. New Media & Society, 16(3), 391-409.

22. Gibson, R. K., & McAllister, I. (Eds.). (2017). New Perspectives on Political Advertising. Temple University Press.

23. Chadwick, A., & Stromer-Galley, J. (2016). Political communication in the digital age: Tools, concepts, and approaches. Routledge.

24. Karpf, D. (2019). Digital politics and political science. Oxford Research Encyclopedia of Communication.

25. Meraz, S., & Papacharissi, Z. (2013). Networked gatekeeping and networked framing on #Egypt. The International Journal of Press/Politics, 18(2), 138-166.

26. Tsfati, Y., & Weimann, G. (2017). Social media and the Arab Spring: Politics comes first. The International Journal of Press/Politics, 22(1), 3-20.

27. Howard, P. N., & Kollanyi, B. (2016). Bots, #StrongerIn, and #Brexit: Computational propaganda during the UK-EU referendum. Available at SSRN 2798311.

28. Tandoc, E. C., Lim, Z. W., & Ling, R. (2018). Defining "fake news"—A typology of scholarly definitions. Digital Journalism, 6(2), 137-153.

29. Persily, N. (2017). The 2016 US election: Can democracy survive the internet? Journal of Democracy, 28(2), 63-76.

30. Kruikemeier, S., Zuiderveen Borgesius, F. J., Helberger, N., & de Vreese, C. H. (2019). Micro-targeting as a tool of political persuasion: Privacy concerns and remedies. Policy & Internet, 11(1), 60-79.

31. Leticia, G. G., & Benoit, K. (2018). Computational analysis of online political communication: Challenges and approaches. In Computational Social Science in the Age of Big Data (pp. 185-201). Springer.

32. Vaccari, C., & Chadwick, A. (Eds.). (2020). Political Communication in the Digital Age: Theory, Practice, and Perspectives. Oxford University Press.

33. Fenton, N., & Barassi, V. (2011). Alternative media and social networking sites: The politics of individuation and political participation. Communication Review, 14(3), 179-196.

34. Boulianne, S. (2019). Social media use and participation: A meta-analysis of current research. Information, Communication & Society, 22(18), 1-24.

35. Coleman, S., & Blumler, J. G. (2009). The internet and democratic citizenship: Theory, practice, and policy. Cambridge University Press.

36. Farwell, J. P., & Shafer, R. J. (2018). Computational propaganda: The new face of communication. Oxford Research Encyclopedia of Communication.

37. Chadwick, A., & Vaccari, C. (2016). Digital politics in Western democracies: A comparative study. Johns Hopkins University Press.

38. Tufekci, Z. (2017). Twitter and tear gas: The power and fragility of networked protest. Yale University Press.

39. Bennett, W. L. (2012). The personalization of politics: Political identity, social media, and changing patterns of participation. The ANNALS of the American Academy of Political and Social Science, 644(1), 20-39.

40. Hindman, M. (2018). Internet politics: States, citizens, and new communication technologies. Cambridge University Press.

www.ingramcontent.com/pod-product-compliance
Ingram Content Group UK Ltd.
Pitfield, Milton Keynes, MK11 3LW, UK
UKHW041954190726
13854UKWH00005B/1968

9 789356 678781